ADD 9573

W9-CMA-620

1g

The Collector's
Book of Jade

Also by Arthur and Grace Chu

Oriental Antiques and Collectibles: A Guide
Oriental Cloisonné and Other Enamels

The Collector's Book of Jade

by Arthur and Grace Chu

Crown Publishers, Inc., New York

Printed in the United States of America
Published simultaneously in Canada by
General Publishing Company Limited

Library of Congress Cataloging in Publication Data

Chu, Arthur.
  The collector's book of jade.

  Bibliography: p.
  Includes index.
  1.   Jade art objects—Collectors and collecting.
I.   Chu, Grace, joint author.   II.   Title.
NK5750.C477   1978   736'.24'075   78-16762
ISBN 0-517-53150-X

Contents

Tribute to a Connoisseur, Collector, and Teacher

On a fine day, when the damp fog has lifted from Chinatown, San Francisco, he emerges from the large old building that serves as his studio and home, in a narrow alley notorious for many bloody murders during the tong wars of the 1890s. His gait is the leisurely one of a Chinese gentleman and scholar; his expensively tailored clothes hang gracefully from his now slightly stooping shoulders. As he waits for the light to change, to cross Grant Avenue, he notes the street sign put up just a few days ago. Beside the old sign, "Grant" in English, is a new one that reads "Do-Pan" in Chinese (DuPont is its English equivalent).

He smiles as he looks at the brand-new sign. Now the light changes. But one does not have to cross like an automaton every time the light shows WALK, particularly if one is taking a leisurely morning stroll. To a cultured Chinese, the motto is always "Take your time"—rushing along is never a virtue. He has long deplored the way so many of the younger generation have lost the "art of living," as Lin Yutang called it. This gentleman's friends have often observed: "Lin extolled the art, but our friend is the personification of it."

The smile remains as he reminisces. Chinatown, his beloved Chinatown, in the past decade has burst its seams with growth. Just look at that pyramid—the Transamerica Building with its needlelike spire—a landmark in architecture, no doubt. But he still prefers the good old days. Take, for instance, this new street sign. Isn't it a good example of Chinese passive resistance? It took nearly a century to produce results, but to the Chinese one hundred years is a short time. As the old saying goes, "It takes a hundred years to plant a tree and let it reach its stature."

The resistance started with a small incident, when Ulysses S. Grant, newly stepped down from the presidency of the United States, decided to visit the Far East. In China he was honored with a banquet fit for a king, but the Chinese failed to provide him with a fork and knife. After repeatedly trying to manipulate the chopsticks and failing to get a morsel of food into his mouth, the former president muttered in frustration, "Can't anybody bring me something civilized to eat with?" The indiscreet remark did not go unnoticed, and word of it soon reached Chinatown, San Francisco. The Chinese were understandably resentful.

The worst was yet to come. The city government decided that the main thoroughfare of Chinatown, which was called DuPont Street, should be renamed Grant Avenue in honor of the first President to visit China. To the Chinese, this was adding insult to injury. In a solemn ceremony, down came the old sign and up went the new one—Grant Avenue—before the eyes of hundreds of unhappy Chinese.

Strangely, the Chinese did not protest openly. They accepted the change with their usual philosophical calm. Of course they would do something—the tried-and-true response, passive resistance, perfected through four thousand years of history. From then on, as one man, they never mentioned the name Grant Avenue. Children just beginning to talk were taught that the name was DuPont Street (Do-Pan Street).* It was the most peaceful resistance movement ever carried out in America or, for that matter, in the world. When anyone asked a Chinese where Grant Avenue was, he got the standard noncommital reply, "I don't know." Or, "Do you mean Do-Pan Street?" That was the only noticeable reaction. But now, after almost one hundred years, passive resistance has succeeded.

"A hundred years is not a long time," muses the gentleman. "Anything takes that long—at least."

Finally he crosses the street because, from the other side, several friends are hailing him. They exchange the usual greetings, and then each moves on to his own business. But he pauses now and then and glances into the narrow side streets. He has spent most of his life in Chinatown. Every street is a reminder of some worthwhile activity in which he has been involved, including several cultural associations—he was one of the founders of the now-flourishing Chinese Historical Society, which presents annual exhibits of Chinese artifacts from early immigrant life. Several streets bring to mind various defunct magazines or publications on Chinese culture for which he served concurrently as editor, feature writer, and—sometimes—messenger boy.

Now the grocery shops are opening. The air is pervaded by the

---

*The Chinese did not really care for the name DuPont, either; it came from that of a well-known or, rather, notorious French bridge. There were many French girls on the Barbary Coast when Chinatown was first settled.

pleasant, familiar smell of bamboo shoots and dried shrimp. Young housewives with shopping bags and older people carrying bamboo baskets begin choosing their daily supplies. From the back of delicatessens come roast pigs, ducks, and chickens, and the butchers chop them on gigantic wooden blocks with sharp cleavers. Delivery trucks filled with crates of live fowl occupy most of the narrow street, where the sidewalk is already overflowing with displays of vegetables and fruits. One rooster, escaping from a crowded cage, flies directly at him, with the delivery man in hot pursuit. The gentleman ducks nimbly. When you live in Chinatown, you have to get used to such small inconveniences.

Soon more people appear on the street, and nearly everyone knows him and greets him. Curio shops are opening too, and many proprietors insist upon showing him treasures they have just acquired. Easily persuaded, but never trying to persuade others, he steps in and waits patiently while the proprietor unwraps his most recent find. Then he saunters along again, though at a slower pace, because he must stop to talk with countless shopkeepers and friends. But what does it matter? When he is ready to sit down and rest, he knows the best restaurant on every street where he can slip in for tea and a delicious lunch, and perhaps find a few congenial friends to reminisce with him.

The gentleman is Chingwah Lee, eminent collector, dean of connoisseurs, expert of experts on Chinese art, and the most beloved person in Chinatown.

Life might have been different for Chingwah Lee. For instance, in 1937, when Metro-Goldwyn-Mayer Studios filmed Pearl Buck's *The Good Earth,* Chingwah Lee was asked to be a consultant, with the title of "technical adviser." He accepted the offer enthusiastically because he felt it would give him a chance to promote understanding of the Chinese as something other than gangsters in Manchu pigtails, chop-chopping their innocent victims. Lee worked conscientiously, and one thing led to another: he was asked to play a part in the film. What a future might have been ahead of him!

At that time, the Japanese war machine had suddenly been turned on China. Millions of helpless Chinese women and children were being massacred, and sympathy for these innocent victims spread throughout the United States. Moreover, Americans wanted to see the barbarous invasion acted out on film, so all the major Hollywood studios needed Chinese actors. They paid them each twenty dollars (remember how much twenty uninflated and undevaluated dollars could buy during the 1940s?) just to make one fall before a Japanese machine gun. (The gunners, incidentally, were also played by Chinese.) Stranded Chinese students, unable to get assistance from their families, flocked to Hollywood on weekends. A dozen falls before the cameras, and they could pay their tuition and board for a whole year.

Had Chingwah chosen to remain in motion pictures, he would be living now in a Beverly Hills mansion. But even though his formal education

Chingwah Lee and Paul Muni in MGM's *The Good Earth*.

Chingwah Lee with schoolchildren on a tour of Chinatown.

Chingwah Lee and Nancy Kwan in Universal's *The Flower Drum Song*.

was Western (University of California at Berkeley; postgraduate work at Whittier, Harvard, and the American Academy of Asian Studies), his Chinese heritage and cultural background were too strong for him to be happy with ostentatious living. He feels more comfortable in a sturdy, roomy house, undistinguished on the outside but filled with Chinese art objects, the finest, the rarest, and the oldest made by Chinese hands—a house only a block or two from his favorite restaurants. (He is also, of course, a gourmet.)

Although Chingwah left Hollywood to pursue his life as a connoisseur, Hollywood never forgot this technical adviser. In the late 1950s when *The Flower Drum Song* was filmed, they again called for his help, and asked him to play a part as well. In fact, he became indispensable, since the location was Chinatown, San Francisco. Through his efforts, Chinatown opened its doors wide for the studio's demands. Chingwah never considers bothersome such interruptions to his sedate life; he enjoys an occasional break, a change of pace. Nor does he consider an added burden such necessary social duties as escorting glamorous leading ladies sightseeing and to fine Chinese restaurants.

There is no place quite like Chinatown, San Francisco—the little colony remains stubbornly Chinese. You can see costumes, furnishings, and other objects that were popular during our grandfathers' days—say, approximately 1860, when Chinese immigrants first arrived in California in large numbers. The artifacts, religious or secular, and the customs that demanded their use had long been out of fashion in China, but in Chinatown even now you can live one hundred years back in time. It is a strange phenomenon that this transplanted culture tends to resist change, yet it is for precisely this reason that Chinatown is so charming and beautiful—a place you want to visit and revisit, a living museum that exists nowhere else in the world. To such a place would Lee naturally return.

The 1930s were a period of uncertainty in China, as the threat of a Japanese invasion drew closer and closer. Chinese families in Peking, Shanghai, and Canton, which had been collecting art treasures for generations, were, for the first time, willing to part with them for cash, to make moving inland easier. Giants of the antiques trade such as C. T. Loo, Yamanaka, and Gump's were bringing treasures out by the shipload. But Chingwah Lee, born with a keen eye for the very best, always preferred to select his treasures one by one, by himself; to handle and study each object lovingly, and become personally attached to it. His was, you might say, a total involvement. It was through this process, and sojourns at various art centers in the Far East, that his expertise became incomparable.

"To know contentment is to achieve happiness," says a Confucian axiom. At heart a Confucian, Chingwah Lee practices all the Confucian virtues: courtesy, loyalty, faithfulness, and, above all, "jen" or "humanheartedness," as it is most appropriately translated by Professor Fung Yu-lan. Confucius also advocated the spread of Chinese ways to edify the rest of the world. Today, of course, this is a presumptuous idea. Lee seeks instead to introduce only the best of Chinese ways to the West. To this end, he delights in showing Chinatown to anyone who shows real interest. Many San Franciscans still fondly recall being taken, during their schooldays, on a tour of Chinatown with Mr. Lee as their guide. With children, he usually achieves an instant rapport. He always has an interesting anecdote to tell about every place to which he leads them, and the children gather closely around him so that they will not miss a word. When they pass the Chinese newspaper office, he stops and looks at the day's paper in the window. "Would you like me to read you what it says? Here it is: 'Mrs. O'Hara's 3rd grade class from Lincoln School is visiting Chinatown today.' " ("To tell you the truth," Lee admitted to us, "even though I always send in the news release, sometimes it doesn't appear in the paper because of too short notice. But all my little guests deserve VIP treatment.")

Before the children leave, Lee invites all of them to his studio for a little talk on Chinese culture. The display of art objects is carefully planned the day before and tailored to the age of the visiting group. So is his talk, which the children find fascinating. He is a born teacher who never forgets that today's children are tomorrow's leaders. (We might mention here that Lee was one of the founders of Chinatown's first Boy Scouts of America troop in May 1914, and is still active in their projects.)

A few days later he usually receives a package of letters, one from each child in the class. "Dear Mr. Lee, I love you. I love Chinatown too. Thank you." Lee chuckles happily over every laboriously printed letter, complete with eraser smudges and pictures of Chinatown in crayon.

Since 1939 people have gathered regularly in his studio on Saturday afternoons to hold informal symposiums. (He has also taught Chinese ceramics, painting, and sculpture at the Rudolph Schaeffer School of Design; incidentally, he introduced Mr. Schaeffer to the collecting of Chinese art.) Many of today's experts on oriental art proudly acknowledge having been tutored by Chingwah Lee, and renowned experts and authors on oriental art frequently drop in to see him. His studio is also open to the public so that people can bring in their treasures for him to appraise. Thus, for almost forty years, Chingwah Lee has acted as unofficial ambassador of goodwill for the Chinese people.

"Mr. Lee," we asked him one day, "after your years and years of collecting, what category of Chinese art excites you most?"

As soon as we spoke, we realized this was not a good question. It is like asking a Chinese father which son is his favorite—number one son? number two? number eight? Naturally, he loves them all.

Lee gave us his famous disarming smile. "My friends, you are asking me if I had four eyes, which two would I use. How can I satisfy you with a simple answer?"

"We'll be more specific—how about jade?"

"Yes, I like jade—particularly archaic pieces. During ancient times, only kings and princes were privileged to possess them. They were used on solemn state occasions. When you hold a piece of archaic jade in your hand, you cannot but feel you are being brought back to the Shang, Chou, or Han dynasties. It truly excites your imagination."

"And the more modern work?"

"Yes, it can have the subtle beauty, the exquisite workmanship, of, let's say, the Ch'ien-lung period."

We were at this time planning to write a book on jade. Knowing that he would not refuse our request, we asked his permission to show in our book selected pieces of his collection. We are grateful for his generosity, and we consider it a unique privilege to dedicate this book to Mr. Chingwah Lee, whose expertise in oriental art will become a part of our heritage.

Acknowledgments

For his help with the Chingwah Lee collection, we want to express our gratitude to Colonel George Fong, USAF retired. George's father was a friend of Chingwah's, and George, a collector of and expert on Chinese ceramics, has, since his retirement, spent as much time with the Old Master as possible. Their close relationship, in our Chinese way, is that of teacher and pupil. George has gone through the many years' accumulation of research material at the studio of the Old Master, recorded Chingwah's comments on his jade pieces, and taken pictures when Chingwah led schoolchildren on his ninety-minute tour of Chinatown. George and Frances Fong, his wife, also edited and checked the details of Chingwah's life story. There is no way we can adequately express our deep appreciation except to say that they are de facto coauthors.

Ann Elizabeth Baldwin patiently sorted the hundreds of slides of Chingwah Lee's collection, taken by Charles Ruiz and Oliver Mills.

We are proud to be able to present two great private collections. The Chingwah Lee Collection encompasses the four thousand years of Chinese jade work; the Foster Collection represents the very best after the art of jade carving reached the peak of perfection. Foster City, California (population 22,491), was so named because it was built by the late T. Jack Foster (1902–68), a man of gigantic vision and achievement. But we must speak of him and his wife, Gladys, as a team, particularly because of their second great achievement, the Foster Jade Collection, which Mrs.

Foster, with characteristic humility, refers to as an "accumulation." The specimens must be termed "monumental." Take, for instance, the mauve, green, and yellow cabbage with green grasshoppers perched on top. The only match to this masterpiece is in the Palace Museum in Taipei, one of the great legacies left by the Ch'ing emperors. "When I first saw our jade cabbage," Mrs. Foster recalls, "I was so overcome that my knees gave way. I simply sank down and stared." Another outstanding piece in the Foster Collection is the jade incense burner from the Summer Palace, formerly in the collection of the famous engineer and metallurgist Daniel Cowan Jackling (1869–1956), bought by him in London in 1906. Mr. Foster literally shouted for joy when he was able to buy the incense burner.

For collectors, Hong Kong is the capital of oriental art and antiques. To us, and many, many others, it is also important because it is the birthplace of *Arts of Asia,* a beautiful and exciting publication that is the work of publisher and editor Tuyet Nguyet (Mrs. Stephen Markbreiter) and associate editor Stephen Markbreiter. Since Hong Kong now receives the best grade of Burmese jadeite and also boasts the most skillful carvers, our book would not be complete and up to date without a chapter devoted to today's jade carving. Chapter 8, "A Master Jade Carver at Work," is taken from a longer article that appeared in *Arts of Asia,* the November-December 1974 issue. We are grateful for permission to use the material, and especially thank Mr. Markbreiter for the original photographs.

Jack Keller and Lewis Scott, the prominent and dynamic dealers in fine antiques in Carmel, California, have given us their generous assistance too, as did our longtime friends Dr. and Mrs. Marvin Hockabout; items from their collection also appear in the book. The names of still other contributors appear in the captions. To all of them, our heartfelt thanks.

Finally, our thanks to our friend and editor, Kay Pinney.

Introduction

A jeweler we have known for a long time recently said to us, "Diamonds may still be a girl's best friend, but jade has certainly become the new sex symbol of the seventies. I've never sold so many jades—rings, bracelets, pendants—modern and semiarchaic. Everybody wants some kind of jade. They'll buy anything!"

"Well, the Chinese believe that jade has magical powers," we replied.

"Yes," the jeweler agreed. "And I know a little about this Chinese *yin* and *yang*, male-female business—isn't that sex?"

"Yes."

"Of course I don't understand the old Chinese philosophy very well even if I do have many Chinese friends. But I love oriental things—I've learned to appreciate lots of the things the Chinese cherish: jade, for one, the 'Stone of Heaven.' I've sold a good deal of that during my thirty years in business—mostly to westerners. A nice bracelet like this"—he held one out that was a third apple-green, the rest glistening white—"I couldn't get fifty dollars for it in the forties or even in the fifties. But look at the price now: five hundred dollars—and I'll probably sell it within the next three days. Why? Because jade, as I said, has become a new sex symbol here in the United States."

Whether westerners have really accepted jade as a new sex symbol, we do not know. But, as our jeweler friend believes, the Chinese have long considered jade a sex symbol in a way—if they ever had one at all.

It is not necessary to understand the yin and yang principle, although a little understanding certainly helps. The Chinese believe that in the beginning there were two elements, the yang and yin, the male and female; and when they united, the process of creation began. However, the two elements do not always combine in equal proportions. Thus, in certain things, the yang or male predominates, and those things belong to the male category. In others, the yin or female holds dominance, and the characteristics of those things will be yin or female. Therefore, within the yin category, there can be a dormant yang element, and vice versa. When the two elements are in correct balance, harmony results. When the balance is lost, disharmony or disaster follows. This is true not only of the sex differences of human beings, which are really at the bottom of the ladder, so to speak, but also of the mountains and the rivers and even the universe itself.

Is jade considered yang (male) or yin (female)? Jade is male, or was so considered by people who provided the raw jade for working into finished products.

In remote Khotan, in the province of Sinkiang or Chinese Turkestan, where most of the best Chinese jade came from, are two rivers called the White Jade River and the Green Jade River. After the jade boulders were washed down from the mountains, they remained in the riverbeds for thousands of years, acquiring added colors from the chemicals in the water, which penetrated the rinds of the stones. These are the treasured jades. Local maidens waded in the water in search of these prized stones. It was considered strictly a woman's occupation. Why did men not compete in this lucrative treasure-hunting? Not because they were lazy, but because of the belief that jade is male and hence could be attracted only by the female. It was thought that even if they had attempted to engage in the competition, men would not have been successful.

In China, since the dawn of history, jade has been regarded as the greatest of all treasures. In ancient times, it was considered to be as valuable as several populous cities. And jades were sometimes traded for cities. Suppose, for example, that a powerful prince ruled our California coast, and he coveted a jade owned by another ruler—say, the ruler of Idaho. His proposal might read something like this: "I offer your highness San Francisco and Los Angeles for your precious jade disk. And if your highness does not consider the price adequate, I will also throw in San Diego as part of the bargain." Thus we can see, jade was equated with power, and in this sense it was a male sex symbol.

Jade was considered to have unusual magical qualities as well. By the Han dynasty (206 B.C.–A.D. 220), the belief had become firmly established that if jade was buried with the dead, it had the power to preserve the corpse and prevent its deterioration. The recently excavated jade suits are good illustrations of this belief. These are shrouds made for the bodies of Prince Liu Sheng (end of the second century B.C.) and his wife. The prince was the elder brother of Wu-ti of the Han dynasty. The emperor was a dynamic ruler who carried on numerous campaigns against the barbarous tribes on the northwestern frontier. His purpose was to keep the trade routes open, but it is also likely that he wanted to keep his court provided with an adequate supply of jade from the region now known as Sinkiang.

One of these jade suits was exhibited all over the world between 1973 and 1975. It was made of 2,156 squares of jade laced together by gold wires. The value of this jade can be put in better perspective if one remembers the arduous effort it took to transport the stone long distances on camel-back over the difficult dry terrain, and the hours spent by dozens of skilled workers, over a period of ten to twelve years, to cut, shape, and polish the jade for the suit (see Ill. 202).

Of course no one except the emperor and his family could afford jade shrouds. Lesser officials and noblemen had to be satisfied with small pieces to cover the seven orifices of the body. These amulets (for that is actually what they were)—among them cicadas symbolizing the resurrection of the dead, pigs for wealth in the afterlife, and many others—have been unearthed in large numbers. When such so-called tomb jades are genuine (at least 90 percent of them are not; but more about them later), they were made during this period.

It was also during this time that Taoism, the philosophy of Lao-tze and Chüan-tze, was transformed into a religion. Its chief aim is to achieve the state of immortality—or at least longevity, and partaking of powdered jade was believed to be one means to that end.

In short, jade has been inseparably tied in with Chinese culture since the dawn of history—as a symbol of power and, finally, as a potion promising immortality. To understand fully the Chinese infatuation with this stone, to feel as the Chinese feel about it, to achieve a better understanding of Chinese culture, it is necessary to explore further not only authentic historical facts, but even folklore, which is also a significant ingredient of a people's national consciousness and heritage.

PART I
Appreciating Jade

1
Stories of Jade

During the earliest times, according to legend, two powerful leaders were contending for the rule of China. After a fierce battle, the good leader defeated the bad, and in despair the bad one threw himself against one of the pillars of heaven (it was believed at that time that the firmament was supported by four pillars, like a large pavilion). The pillar was so violently shaken that it broke, and part of the firmament was damaged.*

When the new ruler came to the throne, he or she (legend does not make this clear) was so saddened by the damaged firmament, which marred the beauty of the world, that she decided to do something about it. Rocks of the finest quality were gathered. But the ruler was not satisfied—the rocks were not beautiful enough. She spent many years in refining them to match the color of heaven (posterity has never learned how this was done).

When the repair was eventually finished and the beauty of the firmament restored, all the people rejoiced and praised their wise ruler. But some of the refined rocks were still left. The ruler had these scattered over the world for later generations to use, to work into objects of beauty and

---

*Another version says that the ruler had fixed the firmament, which was originally imperfect, with five-colored stones, before the pillar was hit and broken by a powerful man called Goon-kun. His blow caused the firmament to crack and the earth to tilt toward the southeast. The legend may represent some terrible prehistoric seismological upheaval that still lingered in the collective memory of the ancient Chinese.

3

beneficence. So it came about that this stone, later known as jade, was called the "Stone of Heaven."

Another legend of the "Stone of Heaven" was the theme of the greatest novel ever written in the Chinese language, *The Dream of the Red Chamber*. During the Ch'ing dynasty, a baby boy was born into a noble family. His birth was received with great rejoicing—it was believed that he would further heighten the already great prestige of the family because he was born with a piece of jade in his mouth. The family named him Pao-yu or Precious Jade.

However, the baby would not stop crying, and the worried family offered a large reward to anyone who could make him do so. Soon a Taoist and a Buddhist monk answered the call. They asked to have the baby brought to them, and then they chided him: "You naughty rock! This is all your fault. Stop that whimpering!"

Strangely, the baby immediately ceased crying. The two priests (representing the two Chinese religions, Taoism and Buddhism) left without claiming the reward.

In the princely mansion named the Garden of the Magnificent View, the boy grew up, loved and protected by his doting grandmother and female relatives, whose company he enjoyed more than that of the scholars and officials, whom he detested. He was facile with rhymes but hated the Confucian classics. His austere father viewed this preference with strong disapproval, because the only way to get a high position at the court was to be able to write a good dissertation in the imperial examination.

The jade that the boy was born with was watched over and protected just as diligently as the boy himself. Twice it was lost and the boy's brilliance became clouded, but each time either the Taoist or the Buddhist monk would find it and bring it back. As a teen-ager, the boy was handsome and became the darling of his several female cousins. (In China, it was permissible—often even encouraged—to marry a cousin on the mother's side, but strictly forbidden to marry one on the father's side.) He loved them all, but his deepest love was for Black Jade, who was a beauty of delicate constitution, much given to melancholy. However, the family wished him to marry another cousin, Precious Clasp, who was also beautiful but of a normal, healthy disposition. Finally the marriage to Precious Clasp was arranged and the date of the ceremony chosen. But by then Pao-yu had again lost the jade, and his intelligence was clouded. He was told he was marrying Black Jade, but the family was able to make the switch to Precious Clasp while Black Jade, whom he thought he was marrying, was dying in a lonely part of the mansion. Strangely, Pao-yu suppressed his grief and took to the study of the classics with diligence. He came out of the imperial examination with high honor, thereby restoring the prestige of the family, which had fallen from royal favor. A promising career at the court seemed inevitable; and his wife was pregnant, thus ensuring another generation for the family. However, Pao-yu did not go back to his family after the examination.

Meanwhile, his father was returning home after a long journey. When it began to snow, he ordered his boat moored so that he could enjoy the lovely scene. Soon three figures appeared in the swirling snow. The one in the middle, in a bright red robe, suddenly stopped, knelt down, and kowtowed. It looked like his son, Pao-yu, but the figure rose and began to go away with the others.

"Pao-yu, Pao-yu, stop!" the father yelled desperately.

Pao-yu turned. There were tears in his eyes.

"What are you waiting for, you naughty rock?" chided his companions, the Taoist and Buddhist priests. "You have cleansed yourself by this incarnation. Don't you want to resume your position in heaven?"

Pao-yu obeyed them. As the amazed father watched, the three disappeared in the snowstorm like a bad dream.

The mythological explanation of the story is that Pao-yu was one of the jades left after the firmament was repaired. Because he showed too much interest in the human world, he was banished from heaven (Taoism) and incarnated as a human being, to suffer the agonies that are part of life (Buddhism). After he had been cleansed by living through the human life cycle, he regained his original position. Of course, before he left, he had to repay the kindness of the family by restoring its prestige and leaving an heir (Confucianism).

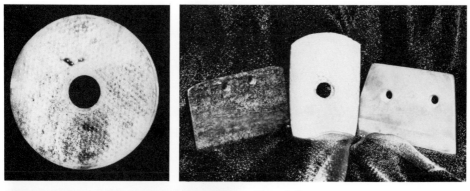

Above left:
1. Jade *pi*, with grain pattern. Early Chou dynasty. *Chingwah Lee Collection*

Above right:
2. Two jade scrapers. Shang dynasty. The axe head in the middle is perhaps conglomerate stone. Neolithic. *Chingwah Lee Collection*

Left:
3. Piece (carved from bone) found in tomb shows as the central motif the earliest of the designs that have appeared later on Chinese jade, bronze, and other artifacts. *Chingwah Lee Collection*

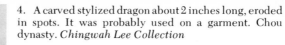

4. A carved stylized dragon about 2 inches long, eroded in spots. It was probably used on a garment. Chou dynasty. *Chingwah Lee Collection*

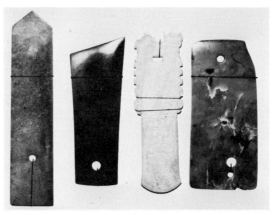

5. Jade symbols. Kuei (*far left*) is a symbol of authority. Axe blade (*third from left*) of white jade is in the form of a tiger. *Chingwah Lee Collection*

6. *Pi*, a symbol of heaven, of translucent green jade. The design represents either grain or silkworms. Chou dynasty. *Chingwah Lee Collection*

7. *Pi* with thundercloud and T pattern. Chou dynasty. *Chingwah Lee Collection*

8. Priests who accompanied the dead to the next world. The two amulets, both from the Chou dynasty, represent the *t'ao-t'ieh*. *Chingwah Lee Collection*

9. Earth tube (*tsung*), 11 inches in height, a very rare piece from the Chou dynasty. Its original pronounced gray green color has turned brown. *Chingwah Lee Collection*

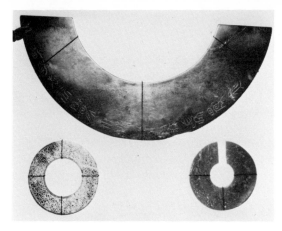

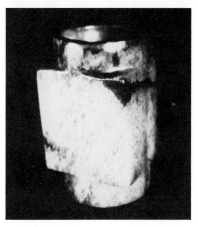

10. *Huang*, 12 inches from tip to tip, dating from the Shang dynasty. The "bird claw" writing was a special style used before the Christian era. Bottom two are Chou dynasty. *Chingwah Lee Collection*

11. Four-sided earth tube (*tsung*) of plain brownish color. Late Chou dynasty. *Chingwah Lee Collection*

In ancient China, the highest ranking and most important person was the king. He was the temporal ruler, and in a religious sense, the son of heaven. The term "emperor" did not come into common use until the Ch'in dynasty (221–207 B.C.).

The Chinese word for king is 王

And the word for jade is 玉*

Compare the two. Even a reader not familiar with the language will at once see the close relationship. The only difference between "king" and "jade" is the small dot at the lower right. It represents the object that the king is wearing. In other words, jade is the precious stone fit for the king and for the nobility of his court.

This is of course true. The king, the Son of Heaven, had his jade carved in several forms and in various colors, for use in different kinds of secular or sacrificial ceremonies. Noblemen also had jades in different shapes and forms, to indicate their respective ranks (see Appendix). The king had a master piece of jade as well, so that when the feudal princes came to the court for an audience, their jades could be checked through the slot in the master jade and no assassin could masquerade as a feudal nobleman and approach the royal person. When the king wanted to send an order to a feudal prince in a distant land, his messenger carried a jade of special design—one to reprimand, another to summon a prince to court, and so on. A messenger could not possibly change the mandate. Nor could the recipient be in any doubt of the bearer's identity because the latter carried with him one of the two halves of a stylized tiger. It would exactly match the one the feudal lord had. This type of credential was referred to as a tally.

Rich and powerful noblemen used jade as personal adornment, perhaps belts inlaid with jade or with jade belt buckles. Also popular were musical stones—an arrangement of jade pieces on strings worn around the waist (see Appendix). When the wearer walked or moved, the stones struck against one another and made pleasant sounds that announced his presence as he proceeded, giving subordinates and servants time to remove objects to make way for him and to assume respectful postures. An equally

*Another explanation is that the word represents several pieces of jade on a string.

important purpose was to give people of equal rank the chance to cease making disparaging remarks or gossiping about him, for in China it was a cardinal breach of etiquette to eavesdrop or to surprise—and thus embarrass—people by putting in an appearance unannounced. Even in later ages, a well-bred person would cough repeatedly before entering a room or hall where friends were gathered.

Jade often played an important role in what we now would call international events, and jade diplomacy can be compared with today's oil diplomacy.

During the period of the Warring States (481–221 B.C.), the Chou dynasty court was greatly weakened, and feudal princes and marquises became veritable rulers of their fiefs. Alliances were made and broken every few months. The ambassadors of the princes daily visited other fiefs to carry out their respective tasks of personal diplomacy. They were the most important men of the time, equipped with knowledge of the world, a quick wit, and a gift of eloquence, and they were adept at playing power politics.

Once the ambassador of Ch'u planned a visit to the dukedom of Chin. To honor the visitor, the duke ordered a state dinner and appointed his own favorite minister to act as the official greeter. Putting on his best jade musical stones, the minister went out to welcome the guest. After the ceremony was over, he ushered the guest into the big banquet hall. Now, during the polite and ceremonious bowing, he had contrived to jangle the jade stones he was wearing. When the expected compliment did not seem to be forthcoming, he remarked casually to the distinguished visitor, "I have long heard of the national treasure of your country, the fabulous white jade. Can Your Excellency enlighten me about its value?"

"No," replied the ambassador. "In our country we do not consider such trinkets as treasures."

"Then pray tell," said the minister, recognizing the rebuff, "just what does Your Excellency consider to be your country's treasure?"

"What we value most are the learned scholars who give wise counsel to our duke, and the wealth of food produced in our great lake region, which nourishes our people. These, Your Excellency, are what our humble country considers as treasures."

Another historical anecdote from the Warring States period concerns an able ambassador and a piece of jade. The powerful Duke of Ch'in sent a message to the Duke of Chao when he learned that this small neighboring country was in possession of a beautiful jade disk or Pi. The message included an offer of fifteen cities in exchange for the jade. This was tantamount to an ultimatum. So the Duke of Chao, after much painful soul-searching, felt that he had to agree. He chose one of his ablest scholar-diplomats, Lin, as ambassador extraordinary to take the piece of jade and go to Ch'in.

The Duke of Ch'in was so pleased that he greeted the guest with great courtesy. After he had seen and admired the jade, he decreed that a

12. Jade knives and scrapers, all meant for ceremonial use. Late Chou dynasty. *Chingwah Lee Collection*

solemn ceremony be held to accept the jade from the Duke of Chao's emissary.

However, that scholar-diplomat began to suspect that the prince had no intention of giving the fifteen cities in trade. Careful observation and inquiry confirmed his suspicions, and thereupon he secretly sent one of his trusted men to take the jade back home.

The next day, before the ceremony started, the ambassador informed the Duke of Ch'in that he was not going to offer him the jade. "Your Excellency," he said, "I have sent one of my retinue back to my country with it."

The duke, scarcely able to control his anger, demanded an explanation.

"Your Excellency," said the undaunted ambassador with great dignity, "I observed after my arrival here that Your Excellency had made no preparation for giving my country the fifteen cities, as agreed. The people in those cities have not been told of the transaction. I therefore decided to send the jade home. If I were to offer it to Your Excellency without getting the fifteen cities in return, I would be guilty of exposing Your Excellency as a man of no faith, a ruler whose promises cannot be trusted by his equals. I decided I could not do such an injustice to Your Excellency."

The Duke of Ch'in immediately rose and apologized profusely to the ambassador.

13. Cylindrical jade that may have been used in connection with astronomical instruments. The erosion resulted from its being buried. Chou dynasty. *Chingwah Lee Collection*

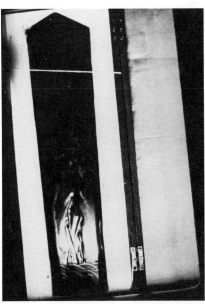

14. *Kuei.* The intended meaning of the design was that all the land and sea under the stars was ruled by the emperor. Under a strong light, this piece of eel-blood red jade shows translucent bright red spots. Chou dynasty. *Chingwah Lee Collection*

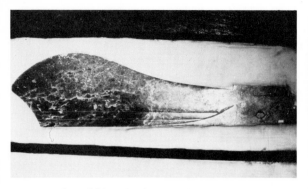

15. *Kuei* shaped like a knife; 12 inches long. Chou dynasty. *Chingwah Lee Collection*

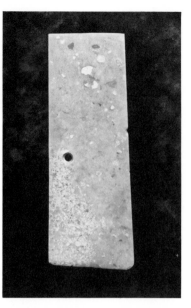

16. Archaic jade tablet, Chou dynasty. *Colonel and Mrs. George Fong*

17. The female figure of a dancer is from the Han dynasty and is remarkable in that it suggests an Egyptian figure. *Huang* (upper left) is from the Chou dynasty; *pi* (upper right), from the Han dynasty. Lower two cannot be dated exactly. *Chingwah Lee Collection*

18. Jade cicadas, called tongue pieces. Such a piece was put into the mouth of a dead person, to symbolize his desire to be reborn like the cicada. Han dynasty. *Chingwah Lee Collection*

19. *Pi*, 10 inches in diameter, with five split-tail dragons in medium relief. Han dynasty. *Chingwah Lee Collection*

Many similar accounts indicate that during the Warring States period jade was greatly valued. Perhaps equally valued was the class of professional ambassadors whose talents and persuasive powers were often greater and more valuable than several armies. They were indeed the Kissingers of yesteryear.

From the above stories we also know that jade must have been very scarce in ancient China. The questions, therefore, have long been: Did China ever produce her own raw jade? And if so, where was it found and in what quantity?

There are two schools of opinion. The first is that no jade at all was found in China proper, which was considerably smaller in area in ancient times than it is today. The raw jade supposedly all came from Turkestan (Sinkiang), which did not become a part of Chinese territory until the Ch'ing dynasty (1644–1912). In ancient times the area was a region of nomadic tribes or of barbarians. When the Chinese government was strong and expansionist, the area was within the Chinese sphere of influence, and the people paid tribute to China, mainly in the coveted stone, jade. However, when the Chinese influence was weak, men from these same regions were likely to be independent and even to raid the bordering Chinese territory. Then the stone had to be bought from these nomadic tribes at exorbitant prices. Regardless of whether it was offered as tribute or bought at high prices, the jade China treasured had to be carried by camel caravans through dangerous arid desert, and it took months to reach China. Most of the raw jade was in the form of huge boulders, as it was found in the rivers, and it was heavy and awkward to carry.

The second theory is that a small quantity of jade was found in China, but because of the great demand, this was exhausted long before the Han dynasty (206 B.C.–A.D. 220). Bolstering this theory is a historical document about the famous "Ho's Jade." The following information is from Hanfei-tze (third century B.C.), founder of one of the famous Hundred Schools of Philosophy:

A man by the name of Ho, in the state of Ch'u, while crossing a small stream found a jade boulder. He hurried back and got a shovel to dig out the boulder and a hand cart to carry it away. It was larger and heavier than he had realized, but after much struggling he succeeded in getting the huge stone on the cart. It nearly broke the boards and it strained the axles greatly, but Ho finally managed to get it home. His friends were curious, but Ho told them that he wanted to give it to the king, and the next day he toiled through the town, pulling the heavily laden cart to the palace gates, saying, "Inside is a jade for the king."

Hearing the commotion at the gate, the king sent a messenger to learn the cause. Upon being told of the jade boulder, he was highly pleased, and immediately instructed his jade carver to examine it. After looking it over, the carver told the king that it was nothing but a common rock. Angry and disappointed, the king had Ho's left foot cut off. But still Ho guarded the boulder as a great treasure. A few years later King Li died and was

20. *a*. Pommel of jade for top of sword. *b*. Sword_ guard piece. *c*. Scabbard hook. *d*. Scabbard hook. *e*. Scabbard end piece. *f*. Scabbard end piece. Chou and Han dynasties. *Chingwah Lee Collection*

succeeded by King Wu. Again, Ho toiled to get the boulder across the city to the gates of the palace.

Like his predecessor before him, King Wu sent for his jade carver and told him to examine the boulder, and this expert too declared it to be just a common rock. Poor Ho—his other foot was cut off!

Many years passed, and eventually King Wu died. He was succeeded by King Wen. The day after Wen was enthroned, he heard great wailing at his gate. Now King Wen was a kind man, and he himself went to the gate. There was Ho with his cart, nearly broken in half by the weight of the stone after so many years. Ho's head was bowed down onto the stone, and he was lamenting in a loud voice.

"Why are you wailing so much?" demanded the king. "I have seen rich and poor with their feet gone, and they did not make such a show of their grief."

"Oh, good King Wen, I am not grieving for losing my feet. I am grieving because I have a beautiful jade, and everybody calls it a rock. And here"—Ho beat his breast and pointed at himself—"is an honest man, and everybody calls him a liar."

At that, the king ordered his carver to come to the gate and cut the stone. After the work had progressed to the point where the stone was ready to separate into two pieces, the king was notified and he returned to witness the fateful moment. When the great boulder was cleft, there indeed appeared a magnificent piece of jade. The highly pleased king, in front of the great crowd that had assembled, rewarded Ho with a place to live on the palace grounds. Most important to Ho, however, was the king's decree that the jade would thereafter be known as "Ho's Jade."

Skeptics have tried to discredit this story. They argue that the earliest Chinese dictionary defined jade merely as a beautiful stone. Hence, the historically famous Ho's Jade might have been just a particularly beautiful stone—perhaps a piece of agate or amethyst. It is true that the early Chinese dictionary—no doubt Shu Wen—did give such a definition. It did not, however, say that *any* beautiful stone was jade. Furthermore, almost all the excavated jade artifacts from the earliest times are of the nephrite variety of jade.

The Chinese seem to have an uncanny ability to distinguish jade from other stones. To them, it possesses that nameless quality that can only be called mystique. It is more than just a precious or semiprecious stone. The instances are too numerous to mention: At least one third of the girls born in China are given the word jade as part of their name—for example, Red Jade, Green Jade, Jade Snow. Boys' names too were so chosen but in such a way as to reflect power or prestige—*Pi* (a jade disk indicating a high rank in ancient times), *Kuei* (a jade scepter), or *Pu* (raw jade, which may contain a jade of great value). The clear and pristine sound of music is referred to as produced by a jade flute. And when two Chinese armies met in battle and one succeeded in besieging the other's city, the standard ultimatum calling for surrender usually ran like this: "If you stubbornly refuse to surrender, we'll make no distinction between jade and ordinary rocks when we enter your city," meaning, of course, that they would destroy everything and kill all the people. The defenders, on the other hand, if they had decided to fight to the last man, would reply in equally appropriate language: "We'd rather be broken jades than whole tiles," meaning, "We have the virtues of jade—courage and integrity."

21. Bound jade tablets. Emperor Hsüan-tsung, T'ang dynasty (A.D. 713–56). *Collection of the National Palace Museum, Taipei, Taiwan, Republic of China*

22. Jade inlaid pieces for the bronze container. T'ang dynasty. *Collection of the National Palace Museum, Taipei, Taiwan, Republic of China*

23. Jade inlaid pieces for the bronze container. T'ang dynasty. *Collection of the National Palace Museum, Taipei, Taiwan, Republic of China*

24. Bound jade tablets. Emperor Chen-tsung, Sung dynasty (A.D. 998–1020). *Collection of the National Palace Museum, Taipei, Taiwan, Republic of China*

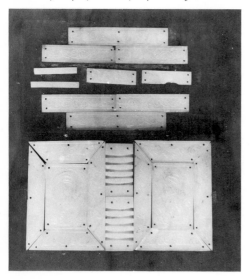

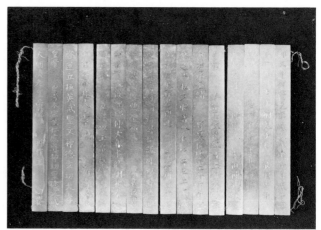

25. The Buddhistic pantheon. The jade is of very uniform olive green celadon color, 22 by 18 inches. Ming or transitional. *Chingwah Lee Collection*

27. Jade bracelets of various designs; Han dynasty and later. *Chingwah Lee Collection*

26. Cabbage with insects, a favorite motif of Chinese ivory carvers; rarely used with jade work because of the difficulty of finding suitable material and of the work involved. All jade lovers know the highly publicized jade cabbage in the Palace Museum in Taiwan; the beautiful specimen in the Foster Collection is making its debut in this book. The chloromelanite cabbage shown here has dark black green upright leaves full of the vitality of growth. Unfortunately, the very dark green tones of this jade cannot be effectively reproduced in color. *Chingwah Lee Collection*

The most solemn ceremony for a Chinese ruler was the sacrifice to Heaven and Earth (*feng-shan*) on the sacred Mount Tai. It could only take place when the nation enjoyed peace and prosperity and was free from any natural or man-created disasters. Theoretically, therefore, not every emperor was entitled to perform the ceremony, although if an emperor wanted to do so, there was no way to prevent him. According to reliable historical records, no more than eight such ceremonies were held from the first emperor of Ch'in, who unified China in 221 B.C., to Sung Chen-tsung in A.D. 1008, the last emperor to perform the ceremony.

The most important objects in the ceremony were the jade books, or tablets, that carried the message to the spirits of Heaven and Earth. Two sets were made, one to be buried near the sacred mountain, the other to be carried back to the palace by the emperor.

In 1933, when the soldiers of General Ma Hung-k'uei were clearing away the rubble of a destroyed pagoda near the sacred mountain, two sets of jade tablets were discovered. General Ma kept the tablets for the duration of the war, but in 1950 he brought them to the United States and put them into the vault of a Los Angeles bank. In 1971, his widow returned these important treasures to the government of the Republic of China.

These tablets had, in fact, been discovered at least once before—during Emperor Ch'ien-lung's reign. He ordered them to be reburied. There were naturally sycophants who told the emperor that he was entitled to the ceremony, to which the emperor replied, "In performing such a ridiculous act, the emperor would deceive himself and cheat the people." On the other hand, perhaps he did not care to go through the seven days' fasting before the sacrifice.

Of the two sets of jade tablets found (Ills. 21–24), the one from the T'ang dynasty has *not* been definitely identified as jade. It is a beautiful white stone, softer than jade and therefore more easily carved. But the one of the Sung dynasty is definitely made of nephrite. The choice of the stone used was dictated perhaps by the differences in spirit between the two periods. The taste of the T'ang rulers was cosmopolitan, broad, and innovative. Under their encouragement, jade carving, as well as calligraphy, painting, poetry—all the arts flourished. The Sung taste was neoclassic and much more restricted. The T'ang emperors particularly liked the art of calligraphy. Given the choice of using real jade at the expense of calligraphy, or using a substitute material to ensure good calligraphic results, they would gladly choose the latter. As the result of this preference, the T'ang tablets, in semiarchaic Li-script, were beautifully done; the Sung set, using real jade material, clearly exhibits the difficulty the carvers had in executing the characters.

What are the virtues of jade? Confucius summed them up as follows:

Like intelligence, it is smooth and shining.
Like justice, its edges seem sharp but do not cut.
Like humility, it hangs down to the ground [like a pendant].
Like music, it gives a clear, ringing sound.
Like truthfulness, it does not hide its faults, which only add to its beauty.
Like the earth, its firmness is born of the mountains and the waters.

Americans today seem to have become infatuated with jade. The prices have risen higher and higher at all the big auctions, and collectors are not only proud of their jade carvings or jewelry, but convinced of the magical quality of jade too. For instance, one real estate executive of our acquaintance keeps a small Chi-lin on his desk. It is carved from gray jade, a fairly old piece. Our friend says he never listens to weather forecasts—he considers them quite unreliable. Rather, he depends on his jade. When its gray color turns ominous, bad weather is coming. He claims the jade has never failed in its predictions.

It might be mentioned here that our friend was not aware of the legend about the jade fish in the Han palace of some two thousand years ago. The tail and fins of that fish would move as if swimming when a rainstorm was approaching.

Another friend of ours was so fond of her beautiful green jade pendant that she never took it off. One day, however, she suddenly became dangerously ill and had to be rushed to the hospital. Before leaving home, she carefully put the jade pendant away because she was afraid she might lose it. When we saw her after her recovery, she told us, "I knew I was very ill because my jade looked so dull and lackluster. Now that I am well, it is bright and sparkling again, so I'm sure I have completely regained my health."

2

The Rape of the Summer Palace

If you step into a prestigious gallery, pause before a carved jade piece, and show more than normal interest—especially if you look as if you are of the monied class—the proprietor is likely to come up and ask, "May I show you this jade, sir?" And as he takes it carefully from the glass case, he may add discreetly, "It's from the Summer Palace."

Even if you are browsing in a third-rate antique "shoppe," you may see a pendant that looks like jade and think it would make a fine birthday present for your wife, who has lately caught the jade fever. And if you and the shoppe owner reach the haggling stage—you offering twenty-five dollars instead of the thirty dollars he wants—the owner may produce his most effective weapon: "This jade pendant is from the Summer Palace. I *paid* twenty-five dollars for it."

What is this Summer Palace, anyway?

It is the name given by westerners to the sprawling pleasure garden or gardens adjacent to the innermost confines of the Forbidden City. Dotted with pavilions, temples, shrines, pagodas, artificial lakes, and gracefully arched bridges, the palace was not limited to summer use; it was a place for relaxation and informal living for the royal family, a place for enjoying festivities and, generally speaking, getting away from the ennui of daily court life. It was also the place where Manchu rulers, such as the emperor Ch'ien-lung and the Dowager Empress, after a long reign, lived out their leisurely semiretirement, surrounded by favorite courtiers and art treasures.

These rulers often spent large sums of money to build new palaces or rebuild extant ones that were already luxurious beyond our imagination, or to add new features to suit their particular taste. The most notable example was the Dowager Empress, who did not think the celestial kingdom she ruled needed a navy, and so transferred the appropriations to the rebuilding of her pleasure palaces. When the work was finished, she gave a magnificent party. Proudly pointing to the marble ships along the lake shore, she laughingly told her guests (among whom was the fidgeting and uncomfortable minister of the navy), "Look, this is my navy!" A few years later, China was defeated and humiliated by her small neighbor, Japan, because the outmoded Chinese ships were no match for Japan's Western-style, cannon-firing warships powered by steam.

The building of the so-called Summer Palace started on a large scale with the emperor Ch'ien-lung, who loved to do everything on a grand scale. He even included in his plan Western-style buildings, following the advice of his favorite Jesuit priests. Perhaps the emperor genuinely needed his numerous lavishly furnished buildings. He is considered, among the Manchu rulers, to have been the most ardent collector of art and art objects, and the additional buildings may have been a matter of necessity.

Jade carvings often form an important part of any Chinese art collection, and the specimens produced in the palace atelier were mostly of the monumental type.* The emperor had just brought into his fast-growing domain Sinkiang, or Chinese Turkestan, for ages the source of Chinese raw jade—nephrite, which the Chinese call "true jade" to differentiate it from the newly recognized jadeite, a more vivid and colorful variety of jade from Burma. Naturally, a jade-loving sovereign wanted to control as much jade-producing territory as he could. But his army had met with near disaster in mountainous northern Burma, and his generals had had to pay Burma large sums of money in exchange for tribute to the Son of Heaven. The emperor, kept in the dark about this secret deal, remained highly pleased that his prestige extended over nearly all the continent. Now he had an unlimited supply of the world's choicest nephrite and jadeite. However, the art of jade carving is so time-consuming that it often took even his master carver half a year to finish an item. In fact, the emperor had to keep his craftsmen working twenty-four hours a day, in shifts, in order to have favorite pieces finished in half that time.

---

*Jade referred to as of the "monumental" type is by no means ten feet tall. In this book, we are using the term to refer to the quality of a specimen—monumental in concept, design, and execution. Such a piece deserves the term "monumental" even though it may be only six, eight, or ten inches tall.

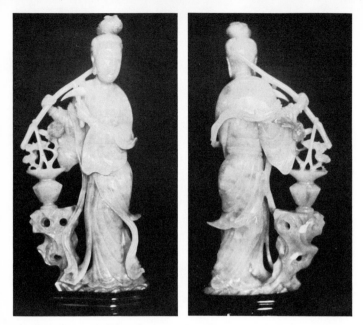

28. Figurine with flower basket and garden tools. The color is mauve, with many emerald green highlights. This was the first jade Mrs. Foster bought—long before she became a serious collector. *Foster Collection*

29. Back view of the jade lady in Ill. 28.

30. A truly monumental vase, over 12 inches in height, of unctuous white nephrite. *Foster Collection*

31. *a. & b.* Front and back views of a seated Buddha, of translucent apple green jadeite. *Foster Collection*

32. Fluted flat dish carved paper-thin in the Mogul style. The gray green jadeite is uniformly scattered with black markings. Diameter, approximately 6 inches. *Foster Collection*

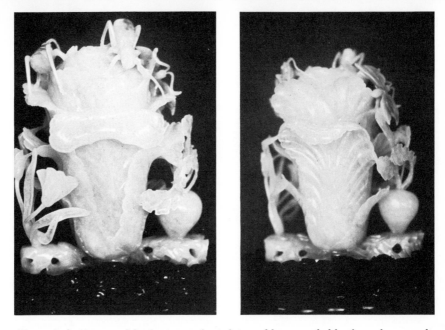

33. *a. & b.* Front and back views of a jadeite cabbage, probably the only example comparable to the one in the Palace Museum in Taiwan. (See also Color Plate 17.) *Foster Collection*

34. Pair of apple green jadeite "cricket cages." *Foster Collection*

35. Jadeite water coup. The vessel and the flowers are deep apple green; the lower floral scroll, chestnut yellow. *Foster Collection*

36. Beauty with a crane; light green jadeite. *Foster Collection*

37. Covered vase with bird perched on top is of uniformly green jadeite. *Foster Collection*

38. Covered jade vessel is light green with brown markings at the foot. *Foster Collection*

39. Pair of fighting cocks; white jade. *Foster Collection*

42. Figure of a Chinese scholar; uniform emerald green jadeite. *Foster Collection*

40. Pale green hanging flower basket with free rings. *Foster Collection*

43. Large light green vessel in the shape of an archaic bronze. *Foster Collection*

41. Large incense burner of pale green with brown markings. *Foster Collection*

44. Figure of Han Hsiang-tzu with flute, one of the eight Taoist immortals. The jade is a uniform light green. *Foster Collection*

45. Lotus flower (symbol of purity) with leaves and roots. Crane (symbol of longevity) is standing under the plant. *Foster Collection*

46. Large covered vase of classic shape is white with traces of green. *Foster Collection*

For any piece that particularly caught his fancy, Ch'ien-lung would compose a poem, write it in his own handwriting, and have special carvers engrave it on the jade. Sometimes, the emperor just composed the poem, and one of his officials who was good at calligraphy would do the writing for him. The famous gigantic black jade wine vessel (four feet, six inches at the rim), which was first seen at the court during the Yüan dynasty (1277–1368) and reported by Friar Oderic of Pordenone in the fourteenth century, later disappeared. Ch'ien-lung rescued it from a monastery, where it was being used as a container for pickled vegetables. He composed three poems to commemorate the occasion and had them inscribed on the old piece.

There were times when the emperor's literary efforts would go too far. He would add his poetry and his name or sobriquet to historically important specimens of archaic jade, ceremonial pieces that had been carved two or three thousand years earlier. To purists and classical scholars, these acts were sacrilegious.

Jade creations carved under the personal supervision of Ch'ien-lung, together with those done in the long reign of his grandfather, K'ang-hsi, who first established the ateliers in the palace for the different arts and crafts, numbered literally in the hundreds. These were displayed all over the Summer Palace (the emperor's name for it was Yüan Ming Yüan). After fifty-nine years on the throne, Ch'ien-lung retired in favor of his son Chia-ch'ing, elevating himself with the title of Grand Emperor.

The fortunes of the Manchu dynasty went into a headlong decline. The main reason was that the Manchus no longer produced strong rulers such as K'ang-hsi and Ch'ien-lung had been. The immediate cause, however, was their lack of knowledge of the outside world and of how to deal with foreign nations. China suffered her first defeat by England during the Opium War, and was forced to cede Hong Kong and pay for the opium that China had confiscated from the British merchants and burned. Next came the 1860 Anglo-French expedition. When the joint foreign armies approached Tientsin, the emperor Hsien-feng fled to Jehol and died there. The Anglo-French forces under the command of Lord Elgin, whose family was noted for art collecting, marched into Peking without meeting any resistance.

For the first time the capital of the celestial kingdom was under the occupation of the "foreign devils." It was a reign of fear and anarchy. The "foreign devils," according to the diary of a court official, soon formed a raiding party. They commandeered oxcarts and other vehicles and headed straight for the Summer Palace. There are various eyewitness accounts to confirm the raid because, in the court's hurried flight, many mandarins of consequence were left in the now-occupied city. Although these important men did not personally dare to watch the "foreign devils" looting the sacred palaces, their servants and cooks did, and reported the outrages to their distressed masters, who, being all scholars and literary men, noted every detail in their diaries, each trying to outdo the others in lamentations and breast-beating. Several of these tours de force were published, and they form the best research material on "the rape of the Summer Palace."

All accounts agree that the raiding party was led by a "foreign devil" with blue eyes (even at that time the Chinese knew that foreigners had blue eyes; but this "devil's" eyes were so blue that they were, to use a favorite Chinese expression, "the color of the sky after a rain.") Moreover, when this "devil" stared at any onlooker, his eyes had the power to make that person tremble and faint as if "an arrow had just been shot through his heart." By the order of this blue-eyed "devil," all the treasures that were once beloved by the great emperors K'ang-hsi and Ch'ien-lung were haphazardly loaded on the commandeered vehicles and carried out of the Summer Palace. Since Great Britain was a seafaring nation, taking booty was considered a legitimate source of revenue of the British Empire. But many members of the raiding party were seen with *their* pockets bulging with the emperors' treasures. These "souvenirs," gradually appearing on the open market, were sold and resold at the big auctions, and even today are labeled as "from the Summer Palace." During the anti-foreign Boxers' incident of 1900, foreign troops again invaded the Summer Palace, and more treasures were carried away. It is therefore literally true that most of the great Chinese jades, particularly those of the monumental type, are now in the Western world!

47. Girl riding a crane is delicately and beautifully carved, with an airy look. *Foster Collection*

48. Chinese beauty with flower branch. *Foster Collection*

49. Two Chinese beauties with a crane, among lotus plants. *Foster Collection*

50. Chinese lady with lotus flower. Jade is a uniform light green. *Foster Collection*

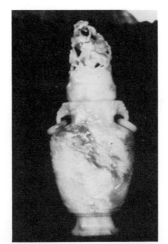

51. Vase with Fo dog on the cover. A good uniform green in color. *Foster Collection*

52. Vase topped with an elaborate floral design is apple green with passages of emerald and yellow. *Foster Collection*

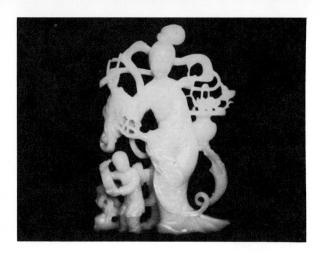

53. Figure of Chinese lady with flower basket; a small boy appears at the base. Apple green. *Foster Collection*

54. Carved white jade teapot. *Stanford University Museum*

55. Covered vessel. Height, about 6 inches. *Foster Collection*

56. Covered jar with figures of boys has a chain of free rings. *Foster Collection*

57. Double gourd with intricate vines and smaller gourds around it. The material, a spotted lapis, makes it appear highly realistic. *Foster Collection*

The blue-eyed leader of the raiding party, however, showed disdain for souvenir hunting and the moblike behavior of his troops. His mission was to punish the heathen Chinese. Before the raiders left, he allowed them to set fire to the buildings. This bit of vandalism was apparently permitted to cover up the shameful behavior of the soldiers under his command, who, being a hastily assembled mob of British and French forces, could not be expected to show any discipline when they beheld the wonders of the oriental palaces.

Who was this blue-eyed man?

He was Major Charles George Gordon—better known as "Chinese" Gordon, for by a strange twist of fate he became the man who actually saved the Manchu empire.

The Manchus at this time (1863) were facing two threats: the joint British and French invasion, already mentioned, and a long-lasting internal rebellion, which posed a greater danger to their very existence. The rebels called themselves the Taipings; they were a quasi-Christian group. The leader, Hung, a converted Methodist, was a native of southern China, where hatred of the Manchus remained strong. Claiming to be the younger brother of Jesus Christ, he organized an army and started a rebellion that shook the whole empire.

When the rebels occupied Nanking in 1853, which of course was long before the Anglo-French invasion and after nearly half of China had fallen into their hands, their quarreling leaders failed to agree upon a follow-through strategy. Hung chose to establish his own Celestial Empire of Taiping in Nanking and declared himself the emperor, but his generals went on independently to continue their attempts to overthrow the Manchus, thus weakening their defensive position in the chosen capital of Nanking.

At that time there were already foreign merchants in Shanghai, with foreign financial interests to be protected. When Shanghai was seriously threatened, the foreigners, along with wealthy Chinese, engaged in the lucrative foreign trade, decided it was in their interest to back the existing Manchu government, from which they had already gained many favors and concessions and hoped to gain even more by their efforts against the rebels. The joint British and French forces were then still occupying several of the important seaports, pending payment of indemnities by the Chinese.

A volunteer army was formed, with the blessing of the Manchu court, which awarded it the name of "The Ever-Victorious Army." But victories were not easy to achieve because this rabble force, mostly mercenaries, had little hope of defeating the battle-seasoned Taiping soldiers unless an experienced commander could be found to train them and whip some discipline into the amorphous group. Unable to find such a capable leader, the Manchu government went to the British for the loan of an officer to command "The Ever-Victorious Army" and save it from ignominious defeat. Major Gordon was suggested, and the post—with the rank of general—was offered to him.

58. Chrysanthemums of white and green jade and coral, with spinach green leaves. The jade planter is decorated with gilt bronze. *Foster Collection*

59. Chinese jasmine flowers of white jade have dark green leaves. Container is white jadeite with passages of apple green. *Foster Collection*

Under General Gordon's command, "The Ever-Victorious Army" became an effective fighting force. The Taiping rebels were routed and forced to surrender city after city. During the last stages of the campaign, it was Gordon's habit to walk at the head of his army with no weapon but a cane. (What Victorian gentleman would go on an outing without his gloves and cane?) In 1864 his task was completed with the surrender of Nanking and the capture of Hung. The Manchu government gave General Gordon the title *titu*, the highest military rank, together with the right to wear the imperial yellow mandarin jacket and the peacock feathers. He rejected an enormous award of money, but kept a gold medal especially struck in his honor by the grateful Manchu government.

Thus ended the legendary exploits in China of Chinese Gordon, the man who first led the raiding party against the Manchu dynasty and permitted the burning of the Summer Palace, but later saved his former enemy from being defeated by the Taiping rebels. His colorful career continued for some twenty more years, however, in other lands, ending in Egypt in 1885.

60. The flowers and berries on this lush plant are white jade. Leaves are dark green; container is shaped like a natural rock. *Foster Collection*

61. Shown here are other treasures donated to the Oakland Museum by the family of the late Dr. Chang Wen-ti (see Color Plate 1). The table screens are set with minutely carved jade panels depicting various Chinese themes. A double rhyton displays sacred mushrooms and other plants. The simple square dish of the finest jadeite needs no decoration. *Oakland Museum*

62. Figure of Shakyamuni as an ascetic is a lustrous light gray green. Late Ch'ing period (A.D. eighteenth–nineteenth century). Height, 10½ inches; width, 7 inches. ASIAN ART MUSEUM OF SAN FRANCISCO. *The Avery Brundage Collection*

This monumental figure is a masterpiece of jade carving and of sculpture as well. The carver's ability to capture the state of spiritual enlightenment of the Buddha can be matched only by the genius of the Ho brothers in blanc de chine porcelain.

63. Covered vase of phoenix design; overall light green jadeite. *Chingwah Lee Collection*

Above right:
64. Jadeite gong (spinach green) carved on both sides. Width from tip to tip, 14 inches. Ch'ien Lung period. *Chingwah Lee Collection*

65. *Jui* (wish-granting scepter) of lilac jadeite. Ca. 1875–1909 (Kuan-hsü). Length, 15 inches. *Chingwah Lee Collection*

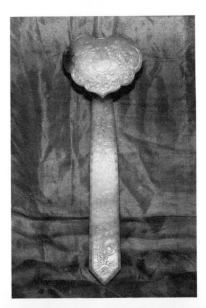

3
Small Jades

Among collectors, we often hear the statement: "I collect small jades."
This may be intended as a polite and modest remark, indicating that the collection of monumental pieces is beyond the collector's means. But such is usually not the whole story. Small jades can be just as costly, particularly if they belong to the archaic category—that is, if they are ritualistic pieces three or four thousand years old; or if they are historically important, having been favorite stones that once belonged to great rulers or eminent scholars; or if the jade has unusual color—mutton-fat jade with tomato red spots or flakes of gold, or a stone with five different colors; or if the jade is not only of unusual color or colors but is carved so exquisitely that—as the Chinese expression goes—"It is the work of the devil." Here, perhaps, is something both East and West can agree on: that the devil is always more clever than a human being.

An admitted collector of small jades seeks a specific type of aesthetic experience, an intimate relationship with his favorite jade or jades. He derives tactile pleasure by constantly feeling its surface, and believes his life enriched by the possession of the beloved object. He may wear it because he believes in its effect as an amulet, for even in our scientific age many people (not just those of Chinese heritage) retain a lingering belief in supernaturalism.

Most monumental jades cannot fulfill this function. They belong to what we now call the category of interior decoration. Not even the most dedicated jade lover would carry around the smallest carved jade mountain on his person. In fact, incense burners, statues of the Goddess of Mercy, or vases carved in the shape of archaic bronze ritualistic vessels have an aloof and forbidding look. Take the case—an extreme one, to be sure—of the jade pagoda of the late Dr. Chang-wen Ti, who spent a good part of his life designing it and then supervising its creation. He could not, even if he wanted to, move it from one room to another more often than two or three times a year. This 51-inch-high, seven-storied pagoda carved from an 18,000-pound apple-green jadeite boulder represents ten years' work by 150 skilled carvers (or the equivalent of 1,500 years by one master carver!). It has been exhibited all over the United States, and during the 1930s and 1940s traveled across the ocean.* After Dr. Chang died, the Chang family donated the pagoda to the newly completed Oakland Museum. (See Color Plate 1.)

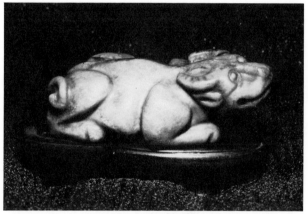

66. Jadeite water buffalo of three colors —tan, yellow, and green. Length, 3 inches. Ch'ien-lung period. *Chingwah Lee Collection*

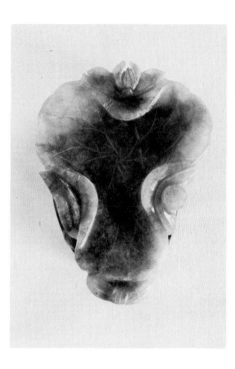

67. Water coup of blue green jadeite in the favorite Chinese design of a lotus plant: curled leaf and flower, bud, seed-pod, and young leaves. The root is carved in relief on the underside. Length, 5 inches; width, 4 inches.

*It was fully insured on these journeys, Chingwah Lee having been one of the appraisers. When the pagoda was damaged in transit, the insurance company was willing to pay only two hundred dollars. Chingwah, outraged, testified for Dr. Chang. As a result, an equitable settlement was reached.

68. A gray nephrite Buddha's-hand citron with ink-black markings. This one has another small fruit and leaves, the favorite design of the Ming dynasty. Length, 2½ inches. Late Ming period.

69. Reverse of Ill. 68 showing leaves, stem, and the citron fruit.

70. Nephrite figurine of the immortal Taoist boy with a string of gold coins over his head. Often he has a three-legged toad as his companion. The figure here was a popular pendant and charm from the seventeenth to the nineteenth century—so popular that half a dozen could be bought any day at the city-god temple market (the equivalent of our flea market today) before World War II.

71. Intricately carved plaque with a crane and peaches in low relief. Symbols of longevity appear at the center. *Thi Antique Jade and Jewelry, San Francisco*

72. Three antique *pi* disks with archaistic designs. *Thi Antique Jade and Jewelry, San Francisco*

73. *Left to right:* antique seal with an animal on top; Goddess of Mercy with a lotus; two double gourds with skin carving of a dragonfly. *Thi Antique Jade and Jewelry, San Francisco*

"Small jades" are not jewels. They do not include bracelets, earrings, cabochons, hair ornaments, and the like. They are created to satisfy the male fancy, with designs of a masculine nature. To use modern terminology, they are certainly symbols of male chauvinism. Take, for instance, the archer's thumb ring (see Ill. 84). This averages about an inch and a half in width and a quarter of an inch in thickness and weighs about three ounces. It can be either round or have one flat side (flat-back) or have a hook to help pull the bowstring. It originated in the early medieval period and was designed to protect the thumb from being scraped by the string when that is released to let the arrow fly. Thumb rings became the favorite awards of the emperor to his generals, and the generals to their subordinates. They also served as gifts between friends. They were worn as symbols of masculinity or sportsmanship even though the wearer may never have shot an arrow in his life.

Imagine a fine autumnal day with a group of Manchurian or Mongolian princes holding an archery contest. Each would gallop on horseback to a marked starting point one hundred paces from the target, a gold coin hung from a willow branch, and with poise and assurance, let the string of his bow glide smoothly over his jade ring, speeding the arrow to the target. Whoever missed the target would receive the penalty of downing three goblets of the potent liquor "mao-tai." It was an occasion to show one's horsemanship and marksmanship, as well as display one's ring.

As a weapon, the bow and arrow now belong largely to the days of our forefathers, and, as a sport, archery has long ceased to be popular, at least among the Chinese people. Yet nearly every collector of small jades owns at least a dozen archer's rings; some who specialize in them possess hundreds in different shapes, forms, and materials, but mainly in jade, and wear a different one each day. Most jade collectors start their collections with a thumb ring or a belt hook, because these small personal items are often well carved and from the finest material. Since jade is almost inde-

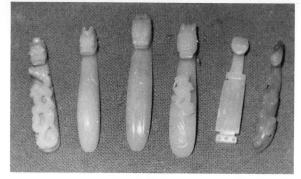

74. Six antique belt hooks. *Thi Antique Jade and Jewelry, San Francisco*

structible and the number of these rings that have survived is almost astronomical, exporters during the 1930s began to seek ways of converting them into articles that were popular with westerners. One such conversion was into little flowerpots for miniature "jade trees" (see Ill. 85); another was making them into souvenir opium lamps. Since westerners had long had a morbid fascination with opium smoking, the little lamps sold particularly well.

Wearing such a ring when it is not actually needed can amount to a small torture, since it is not only bulky and heavy but acts as a straitjacket for one's thumb, restricting movement as well as blood circulation. However, the discomfort gives the wearer the excuse to take it off, examine it, and then put it on again. The ring has long lost its functional value. Yet its obsoleteness seems but to increase its mystique.

Belt hooks are another popular collectors' item (Ill. 83). There are two types of belt hooks—the single-piece and the double-piece type. The single kind was first made during the Chou dynasty, and it was fashioned from jade, bronze, or inlaid bronze. The hook takes the shape of the head of a "ch'ih" (variously translated as an immature dragon, or hydra). On the reverse side there is a button, to be secured to the leather, metal, or fabric belt or girdle. The double-piece type has two sections, one (with the same dragon head) serving as the hook, the other serving as the catch for the hook. Both parts have buttons on the reverse side, so that one part can be attached to each end of the belt. When the two pieces are in place together, they form a well-matched rectangle or square. These belt hooks are often fancifully carved in high relief or in openwork. They form a unique and special category for the collector, although as functional items they too have been superseded by more efficient modern counterparts.

During the 1900s when the export of antiques became big business, many small jades of this kind were shipped into Western countries. Of course westerners did not understand or appreciate the Chinese tradition

75. Five sword hangers with archaistic designs. *Thi Antique Jade and Jewelry, San Francisco*

76. Three beautifully carved antique jade pieces of fine-quality material. *Thi Antique Jade and Jewelry, San Francisco*

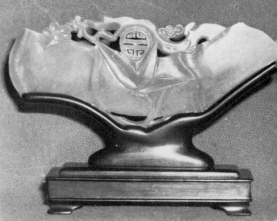

77. A branch of plum blossoms resting on a section of bamboo with the character "longevity" in the center. *Thi Antique Jade and Jewelry, San Francisco*

78. Two jadeite Chinese ladies, one sitting on a garden stool with a flower in her hand. The stone is opaque but of a good mauve and green color. The unsophisticated carving technique shows that it is a product of the 1950s, when most Hong Kong carvers had not completely mastered the art. *Dr. and Mrs. Marvin Hockabout*

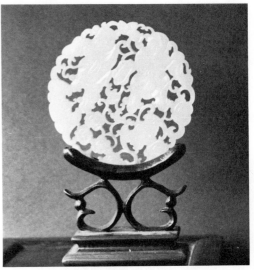

79. Beautifully pierced disk of mutton-fat nephrite. *Dr. and Mrs. Marvin Hockabout*

80. *Left:* Intricately carved contemporary lapis snuff bottle. *Right:* Agate snuff bottle from about 1910. *Dr. and Mrs. Marvin Hockabout*

81. Contemporary snuff bottles of (*left to right*) rose quartz, malachite, and carnelian. *Dr. and Mrs. Marvin Hockabout*

82. *a.* Front view of a double belt hook of mutton-fat nephrite. *b.* Back view shows the buttons that are to be attached to a belt of leather or fabric.

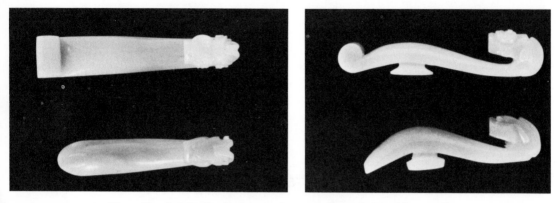

83. *a.* Two belt hooks. One at top is mutton-fat nephrite with a scroll end; bottom one is smoky brown on the lower end. This type of belt hook almost always has a dragon head. *b.* Side view of belt hooks, showing the buttons for attachment to the belts.

84. Archer's thumb rings. *Left to right:* Mutton-fat nephrite; smoky yellow nephrite with one flat side (called a flat-back); gray with ink-black splashes and two incised galloping horses.

Right:

85. Miniature jade tree with jadeite leaves and flowers of coral, turquoise, and greenish white jadeite. The pot is a nephrite thumb ring finished with a repoussé silver bottom and a flange of silver around the top.

86. Belt hooks suffered the same fate of conversion during the great export age of the 1930s. Here, in a tour de force attempt, a hook became the handle of an enamel ashtray.

behind them. Just as happened with archer's rings, the Chinese exporters soon figured out means of transforming belt hooks into objects that would offer more attraction to westerners. The single belt hooks were often made into handles for boxes. This trend was reversed after the 1950s, when Chinese-made items were no longer allowed to enter this country. People began to rescue these jade objects from such various spurious contraptions, just as they have done with the many high-priced porcelain vases that were made into lamps.

Small jade animals form yet another important category. Among them are the twelve zodiac animals: the rat, cow (often represented by the water buffalo), tiger, hare, dragon, snake, horse, ram, monkey, rooster, dog, and pig. As each year is represented by a zodiac animal, a man would carry his own zodiac animal as a good-luck charm.

There are other animals associated with auspicious symbols. The deer stands for longevity, the bat for good luck, and so on. And the plants—first of all, the sacred fungus or ling-chi, associated with good health and other magical virtues; a gnarled pine trunk with its branches in relief over it, or a section of bamboo with a few leaves around it. Both the latter are symbols of sturdiness and the ability to withstand harshness and, therefore, to overcome bad luck. Of the fruits, by far the most popular are the Buddha's-hand citron and the peach. With the ingenious use of the varied colors in the raw material, jade workers can create very lovely decorative pieces in these categories.

Scholars or literary men often prefer jades of archaic shapes and forms. Although not really the creations of thousands of years ago, they are faithful copies: the *pi* (Ill. 6), a circular disk with a hole in the center; the cicada (Ill. 18), universally a symbol of resurrection; and so on. Of course authentic archaic pieces are the most esteemed, avidly collected, and highly priced. They are too rare and precious for the collector to carry on his person.

And we must not forget jade snuff bottles. Because of its toughness, jade is a particularly suitable material for them. Snuff-taking became fashionable during the Ch'ing dynasty, reaching its peak in the affluent Ch'ien-lung period. It was the habit of courtiers to tuck a snuff bottle inside the "horse-hoof" cuff of their official mandarin garment (see Ill. 89). The chic thing to do was to dish out a small amount of snuff with the ivory spoon attached to the stopper, elegantly deposit it on the thumbnail, and with a quick sniff, absorb the entire pile of fragrant powder. The courtier's daintily manicured thumbnail remained as clean as a whistle—and back into the cuff went the little bottle.

Naturally, a snuff bottle was subject to being dropped. A glass bottle would break to pieces with the first fall if it was not made with very thick walls. Ivory and porcelain bottles were also easily damaged, but a jade snuff bottle could stand many falls and still remain undamaged and unchipped.

In the old days a snuff bottle as a rule had a matching saucer. The two parts have usually parted company over the years, and today's collector rarely finds a bottle with its correct saucer. Some collectors like to have a new one carved to match the bottle. The saucer served a very specific purpose: the owner, particularly when he was giving a dinner party, would empty half the snuff onto the saucer, and then pass it around so that other guests could sample the concoction supplied by his favorite maker, who mixed the tobacco and fragrant herbs from a secret formula.

Since many snuff bottle owners are also jade fanciers, the bottles —particularly the expensive ones—usually display the imagination and creative genius of jade carvers. The preferred shapes and forms are fruits—peaches, lichi, Buddha's-hand citron, and so on, preferably with the color of the stone suggesting the real thing.

87. A large carved bronze box with a jade belt hook for a handle. *Colonel and Mrs. George Fong*

88. Jade mouthpieces for pipes. *Left to right:* end piece of—perhaps—an opium pipe; cigarette holder; mouthpiece for a short stubby pipe; end piece for an opium pipe. The Chinese believed that jade powder helped one achieve immortality (or at least longevity). Thus, jade bowls and cups (rhytons), as well as pipe mouthpieces, were favored in the hope that the essence of the jade would be continually ingested.

89. The "horse hoof" cuff of a mandarin robe was just the place for a little flask-shaped snuff bottle.

90. *a.* Rainbow-shaded snuff bottle. *b.* Jadeite snuff bottle with unusually intense patches of bright green, yellow, and light green. *Chingwah Lee Collection*

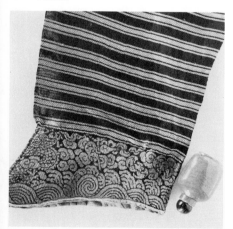

92. A girdle pendant or pocket jade of mutton-fat nephrite in the shape of a small double gourd over a large one.

91. *Pi* or disk with a design of bats, another favorite motif (because the bat is a rebus signifying good luck) of the late Ming and early Ch'ing periods. This disk is of chicken-bone color because it has been in a fire. Eighteenth to nineteenth century.

93. Cicada of low-quality nephrite, showing a great deal of handling and many small chips. Made perhaps about 1900. Cicadas, symbolic of resurrection, have been carved in the thousands throughout the ages, and particularly in recent years.

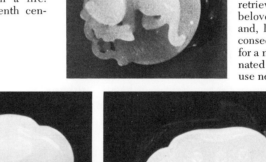

94. A cat napping on a cool palm-leaf fan much needed by its master to relieve his own discomfort. Should he retrieve his fan to cool himself, or let his beloved pet keep its comfortable mat and, like a benign master, suffer the consequences himself? A perfect motif for a netsuke (although the toggle originated in China, the Chinese did not use netsukes).

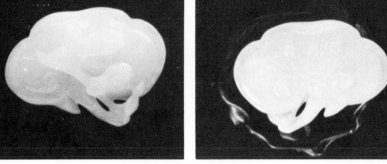

95. *a.* A *ling-chi*, or sacred fungus, made of unctuous pure white nephrite of the finest quality. The *ling-chi* was considered the quintessence of nature and an emblem of good health, longevity, and intelligence. *b.* Reverse of the *ling-chi*.

96. A mutton-fat nephrite cup with one side showing a patch of brown because of age. The design on the outside is an Indian lotus scroll, a popular Ming motif. The handle bears the favorite Sung design of a tiger face on the nearly flat top. Middle to late Ming period. Diamater, 2½ inches; height, 2 inches.

97. Belt hooks with archaistic designs. *Thi Antique Jade and Jewelry, San Francisco*

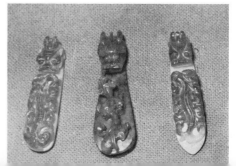

The demand for snuff bottles is greater than ever, even though the snuff habit itself is passé. Collecting the bottles has become a status symbol. Like Japanese netsukes, snuff bottles have become an art form, and skillful and talented carvers are turning out fanciful bottles for collectors, who never question whether they have ever been used as snuff containers. For the carvers, the reward is handsome. For instance, a beautiful jade miniature vase with high relief design would fetch, say, two to three hundred dollars. But if the vase is carved in flask shape (slightly flattened) with the same design as the miniature vase, and a top and spoon are added, the price could be as high as two thousand dollars.

For the purist who will not accept anything but the genuine, the only guide is to find a snuff bottle that was meant to be functional. It should be easy to take out and put back into the sleeve cuff or the pocket without tearing the material of the garment. Therefore any excessive virtuosity of carving is a sure indication that the bottle was made for the collector instead of the snuff-taker.

There was no specific place where small jades were worn. It was purely a matter of personal preference. Some Chinese liked to wear their jades under their jackets, where the stone could be easily reached and fondled. Others liked to hang them on the girdles. Still others kept one in their pockets. It was interesting, in the old days, to see two friends who had not seen each other for some time suddenly and unexpectedly meet at a street corner. After a great deal of ceremonious bowing came the crowning friendly act: each invited the other to admire and fondle his jade or jades.

Small jades, however, do not have to be carried on the person of the owner. A scholar who spent most of his time in his study might have preferred to set them on the desk before him, among his books, brushes, and inkstones. And there are also jade brush rests, jade water coups or water droppers, and jade brush handles. When the scholar was tired of studying or had run out of inspiration in composing poems, or when he was searching for the proper word and could not think of it, he would look at his jades and fondle them. This might reinvigorate him for study, help him recapture his inspiration, and find the proper word for the expression of his ideas.

98. A plaque with a peony and its leaves in relief.

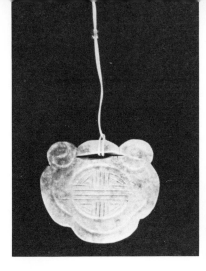

99. A nephrite hundred-family lock. When a baby was born, its mother's family collected money from friends, neighbors, and relatives to buy a lock (often of silver or perfunctorily carved jade) for the baby to wear so that its soul would be locked to its body and no devil could steal the soul. The hundred families contributing toward the lock, plus their legions of ancestral spirits, would defend the baby from evil forces. These collections were happily subscribed to, and reciprocated.

100. Hare of white jadeite with a slight shadow of lavender on the underside. The eyes are red carnelian. Length, approximately 3 inches; height, 1½ inches. *Chingwah Lee Collection*

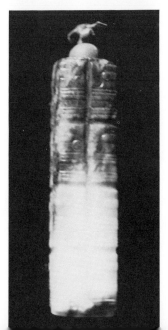

Above left:
101. Snuff bottle in the shape of a bamboo shoot, light green with a yellow brown tip. Length, about 3 inches. *Chingwah Lee Collection*

Above right:
102. Bamboo shoot snuff bottle, light green with brown at the roots. The stand is made of two types of wood. *Chingwah Lee Collection*

Left:
103. Antique girdle pendant of nephrite, cream-colored with brown markings. Length, 3 inches. Ming period. *Thomas Yee Collection*

104. Dragon girdle pendant of yellow nephrite with brown skin-carved dragon. Length, 2½ inches. Early Ch'ing period. *Thomas Yee Collection*

105. Dragon belt buckle of white nephrite. Width, 2 inches. Ch'ing period. *Thomas Yee Collection*

106. Jade box of white nephrite. Diameter, 2½ inches. Late Ch'ing period. *Thomas Yee Collection*

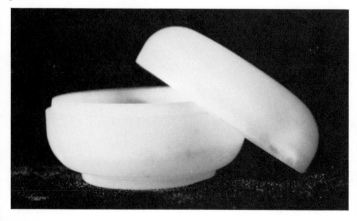

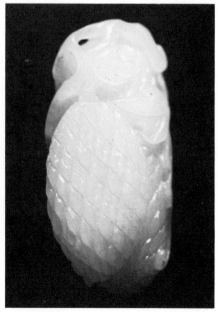

107. Jade lichi pendant of white nephrite. Length, 2 inches. Late Ch'ing period. *Thomas Yee Collection*

4

Jade Flowers

Cheng Te-k'un, the eminent Chinese archeologist, wrote with exhaustive scholarship on a seemingly small subject, namely, *Jade Flowers and Floral Designs in Chinese Decorative Art.** However, the subject is perhaps not as small as its title suggests, for these delicate little carvings span a period of almost two thousand years, from as early as the Warring States period (481–221 B.C.) to the present century. They are not exactly jewelry; the central attraction of jade jewelry is one or more pieces of precious stone, flawless gems whose beauty and value can be destroyed by excessive carving or even faceting. The greatest attraction of jade flowers, on the other hand, lies in the craftsman's virtuosity in carving and piercing. The material used may not be the best grade of jewel jade—it frequently has flaws, cracks, unwanted colors, and other imperfections. But by the clever use of his skills, the carver can often eliminate the flaws and cracks and turn the unwanted colors into an advantage—perhaps into a spray of white flowers with green leaves and brown stem. Some collectors specialize in these small items, and so it seems worthwhile to devote a short separate chapter to the subject of jade flowers.

From the earliest times, because of its intrinsic beauty and its purported power to enhance the health and well-being of the wearer, as well as to dispel evil influences and disease, jade became the preferred material for

---

*Hong Kong: The Chinese University of Hong Kong, Carlson Printers, Ltd., 1969.

personal adornment. Naturalistic designs began to appear in the form of flowers or floral designs and of birds admired for their singing or their plumage. Mythical animals such as the Chi-Ling (unicorn) and the fung-huang (phoenix) were equally favored subjects. These were used as ladies' hair ornaments, earrings, pendants, buttons, or objects to be sewed onto garments. The T'ang dynasty (A.D. 618–907) was noted for its affluence. Besides gold and silver ornaments that were incised and carved into elaborate designs, jade flowers and other decorative items also became common. Although these are small and perhaps insignificant objects, no work or technique was spared because they were intended for the ladies of noble and rich families whose fancies were difficult to satisfy.

Take, for example, the legendary beauty Yang Kuei-fei (Yang, the Imperial Consort), or Jade Circlet Yang. It was said by the famous poet, Po Chü-i, that of the three thousand beauties in the palace, she was the only one beloved by the Emperor Ming of the T'ang dynasty. She wielded such power at the court that all her brothers and nephews and cousins were given the rank of marquis. Not only was she the pacesetter of female fashion at that time; she also gave the whole nation the new belief that the birth of a girl could be a greater blessing than that of a boy. Eventually, her nepotism and love of luxury precipitated a rebellion, and the emperor was forced to flee with his court.

Before the royal procession set out on the arduous mountain route to Szechwan, the bitter and suffering soldiers, blaming Yang for all their troubles, refused to accompany the court unless she was executed. The brokenhearted emperor had no choice. A silk scarf was given to Yang and she hanged herself with it. Her gold and jade jewelry was strewn around her body, yet such was the hatred for her that no one wanted to pick up her jewels.

Years later, when the rebellion was put down and the emperor returned to the capital, he could not forget his beloved consort. He summoned a renowned Taoist to communicate with her spirit, and the Taoist searched through heaven and earth. On Pung-lai Mountain, the Taoist happy land, he located her—she had become an immortal. She told the Taoist to give her love to the emperor, and to tell him that even in the happy land the days seemed tediously long without his companionship. Before taking leave of her, the Taoist asked for some token, so that the emperor would believe him.

"Take this"—Yang broke her gold hair clasp, inlaid with jade flowers, into two pieces and gave him one—"to His Majesty, and I'll keep the other half. Tell him that if our hearts remain constant and true, like the gold and the jade, we shall meet again either on earth or in heaven. As further proof, remind him that on the seventh day of the seventh moon, we made a solemn pledge that we would forever be born and reborn as lovers. This pledge was known only to him and to me."

So ended the tragic story of the T'ang dynasty beauty whose elegant hair ornaments were admired by Chinese women for centuries thereafter.

Great advancement in carving techniques was achieved during the

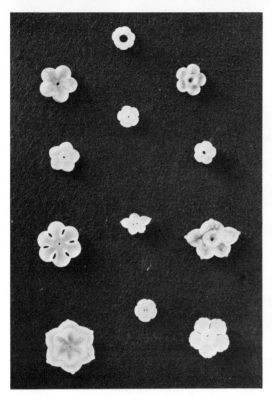

108. Jade flowers, nephrite. Most are white; a few are light celadon. Some are quite old, showing signs of burial and damage.

109. Jade flowers.

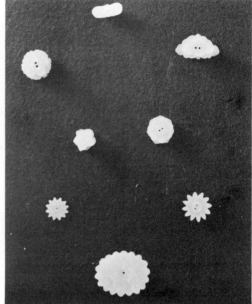

111. Floral designs.

110. Jade designs in human and animal forms.

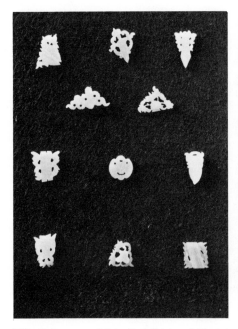

112.   Jades carved into Buddhist and Taoist emblems.

113.   Fruits and *ling-chi* (sacred mushrooms).

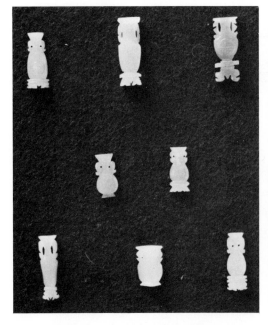

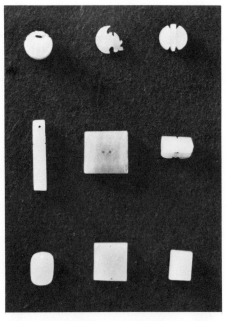

114.   Designs of various forms of miniature vases.

115.   Jade seals. These were worn only as decorations; owing to the difficulty of carving them, they were almost never marked with characters.

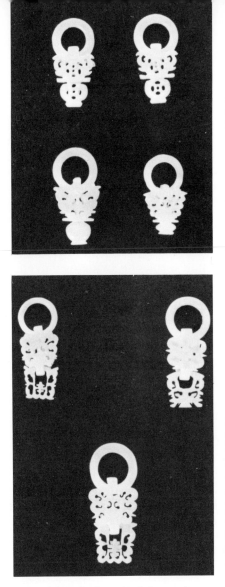

116. Pierced and carved flower baskets with loose free rings. Each free ring takes three days to carve and another three days to polish.

118. Jade characters. The top five characters mean good fortune (*fu*); the two at bottom mean longevity (*shou*). The top piece is serpentine; the large piece beneath it at left is bowenite; the two characters at bottom are jadeite. Remainder are nephrite.

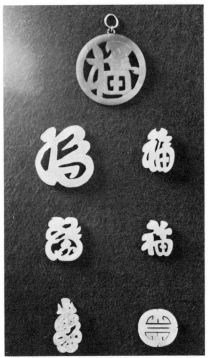

117. Flower baskets. Each hangs from a free ring and has a freely swinging floral plaque beneath it.

Sung dynasty (960–1279). Designs became more elaborate, and jade items began to dominate the field of ornamentation. The Yüan (1277–1368) and Ming (1368–1644) dynasties saw further sophistication in this art. The emphasis was on the method of piercing. The elaborate openwork deserved the term "devil's work," reserved for the type of workmanship that human hands seem hardly able to achieve. So much advancement was made that beside these delicate, airy, feather-light marvels, the T'ang specimens look clumsy and unnecessarily heavy and bulky. The popularity of jade flowers has remained unchanged down to the present century.

From the early times to the eighteenth century, the favorite material was nephrite: the gray-white, the white with a slight tinge of celadon, and the mutton-fat, the most treasured of all.

How these jade flowers were used can be determined by the holes or perforations in them. Those with one hole through the center could be attached in a fixed position to a garment, with perhaps gold or silver wires as added elegance, or to other larger pieces in an ensemble to form a glittering headgear—for instance, the bride's headdress or those of the Manchu noble ladies. Pieces with two or more holes were sewed onto garments—along the hem, around the neck, and down the front. Those with tunneled holes on the reverse side of the flower (holes started from two opposite positions, then slanted downward to meet each other) were designed to hide the thread. Those with off-center holes were made to hang loosely, as on ear drops. (The poetic term "swinging with the steps of the golden lilies" was used to describe their graceful swinging movement as the wearer walked.) Gold or silver hairpins were often adorned with jade Buddha's-hand citrons or simple elliptical knobs (see Ill. 132). Unfortunately, the term for them is rather prosaic—they are called "jade head scratchers." (It was more elegant for a lady to pretend to rearrange her hair and at the same time take advantage of the process to scratch her head.) Another type is equipped at one end with an ear spoon—a tiny spoon to remove ear wax. An elaborate hairpin can be entirely carved from jade —all six or eight inches of it, with intricate pierced floral patterns. Some were encrusted with rubies and other precious stones in inlaid work. These, perhaps, influenced by Indian art, were made from Ch'ien-lung's time or after, when the emperor ordered his jade carvers to imitate some of the styles of the Indian lapidary work as a novelty. Thus were created thinly carved jade pieces with inlays of precious stones.

As mentioned before, jadeite began to replace nephrite as jewel material during the eighteenth century. Jadeite was discovered at some time during the Ming dynasty. The reason several hundred years passed before its intrinsic beauty and potential were recognized was the Chinese suspicion that anything different from the jade they had known since history began must therefore not be a true jade. At first, jadeite was prohibited from being sold as jade. Then, to distinguish it from "true jade," it was called Yunnan jade, which carried a disparaging connotation.

Yunnan borders on Burma—in fact, in the mountainous region, there was no exact boundary line between them. As legend has it, jadeite was accidentally discovered there by a Chinese peasant who made his living selling his produce to the Burmese. Every day he carried his vegetables in two baskets on a bamboo pole balanced across his shoulder. One day he failed to sell all his goods, and still had one basket full. It was getting late. He had no time to rearrange his goods so that their weight would be balanced for easy carrying. Instead, he picked up a boulder and put it into the empty basket, then hurried across the border to his home. The next morning, noticing how beautiful the boulder was, he took it to a jewel-stone cutter. The lapidary identified it as jade and bought it from the peasant, paying a good price. Soon the news began to get around that jade had been discovered, and many people began to travel across the border to search for it.

Almost all jadeite flowers were made during and after the eighteenth century. However, nephrite of the mutton-fat variety, for the reasons we have mentioned, continued to be made into jade flowers. All these little gems are an important and almost independent branch of Chinese jade carving.

To writers on Chinese art and antiques, it is always distressing—after familiarizing their readers with the "beautiful things" that the Chinese have produced—to point out that these things are not available any more, or can be bought only at exorbitant prices. Thus, we are especially happy to end this discussion on an upbeat note: Since the government on the Chinese mainland frowns on collecting (one of the charges against Liu shao-chi during the power struggle called the Cultural Revolution was that he collected antiques), and since the government called upon the people to contribute their jewelry to the nation—gold, silver, and jades—it had in storage a great quantity of small items, which are now being sold at the Canton Trade Fair, where twice a year foreign merchants are allowed to buy whatever is offered for sale. Jade flowers are among the items offered. Many are slightly damaged, but they show exquisite workmanship. Some are truly old ones; nephrite objects are practically indestructible, so it is very difficult to tell exactly how old they are. Large numbers have been brought back from Canton by dealers who attended the fairs. If collectors look carefully on the market, they will be able to find jade flowers at very reasonable prices.

119. At center is a pierced figure of the God of Thunder (*kuei-hsing*), also the God of Literature. At center left is a grape cluster; to the right, a jade bat. At the four corners are jade birds.

120. A floral plaque carved in three layers.

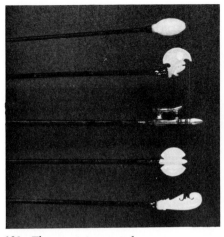

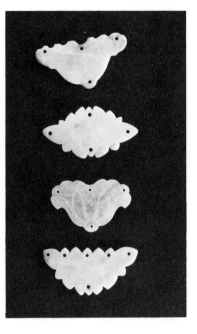

121. These miniature jade weapons were probably made for a miniature shrine of Kuan-yu, the God of War.

122.   Large jadeite lotus flowers and leaves.

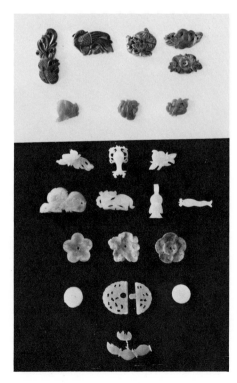

123. Various pieces of carved stone in familiar Chinese designs. The group at the top is malachite; the second row, carnelian; the others are nephrite.

5
Jade for Jewelry

Although the Chinese have used jade for jewelry or, in a more general sense, for personal decorative items for nearly four thousand years, westerners have not fully recognized its potential as a jewel. They have used a different set of standards to judge the quality of a jewel stone—its transparency, luster, ability to refract and disperse light, its purity and uniformity of color, its hardness. Diamonds, rubies, sapphires, emeralds, and the like are valued according to these characteristics. Also important is the faceting that brings out these qualities. Westerners did not appreciate the subtle beauty of translucent or near-opaque stones like jade, or the variety of color tones half hidden in a "now you see it, now you don't" way, like the face of a shy beautiful girl seen behind a veil. They ignored the texture and the pattern of colors—and their harmonious blending, such as is found in "the moss in snow," the rare mutton-fat with blood spots or specks of gold. This is not to say that solid colors of jade are inferior. Among the choicest are the vivid green likened to a pool of still autumnal water, and the mauve or pinkish purple as tender as the blush on a youthful cheek.

The fourteenth-century connoisseur Ts'ao Chao, in his *Ko Ku Yao Lun* (*The Essential Criteria of Antiquities*), which has been ably translated into English by Sir Percival David, divided jades into several categories according to their colors: white—that with mutton-fat color is the most valuable; yellow—the color of roasted chestnut kernels is the choicest

51

and smoky yellow is next; dark blue green—the color of indigo is the best, that with black spots or of a lighter color being less valuable; black—lac-black or ink-black is not very valuable; red—jade as red as a cock's comb is very difficult to find; green—the deep color is the best, the lighter shades less valuable; spinach color (a not too pleasant blackish green), the least valuable of all.

Ts'ao Chao was writing about nephrite, which during his day was considered to be the only true jade. Because of its toughness or unbreakable quality, nephrite can stand the severest kind of intricate cutting. The fanciful carving of flowers and floral patterns enhanced by freely swinging loose rings became a unique branch of jade art. But nephrite has a hardness of only 6 (some mineralogists put it as low as 5¾), and so it does not stand wear well. Quartz, which is a very common mineral, has a hardness of 7, and dust contains a large number of minute quartz particles. Nephrite, therefore, cannot stand the daily abrasive action of common dust. Nephrite bracelets or the cabochons of rings, if worn constantly, will need to be polished or resurfaced often. Used as a pendant, necklace, brooch, or hair ornament, however, nephrite cannot be excelled in overall durability. And imagine the dramatic contrast of an intricately carved white mutton-fat jade hairpin against the raven black hair of a Chinese beauty!

Even during the Ming dynasty, when Ts'ao Chao wrote his important opus, jadeite was not recognized as true jade. During the eighteenth century, it was finally accepted as a different kind of jade. Not only that, but its exciting colors had gained for it great popularity for jewelry. It has a hardness of 7—as great as that of quartz. It has all the colors of the

124. Necklace of jadeite beads. It is of a uniform light apple green color, and very translucent. *Colonel and Mrs. George Fong*

125. Necklace of jadeite beads of reddish brown, lavender, green, white, and black. Faceting on jade beads is a feature newly adopted by Far Eastern lapidaries.

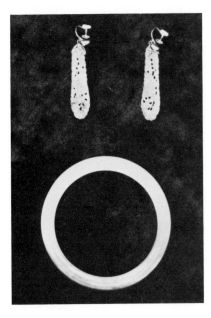

126. Pierced jadeite eardrops and a jadeite bracelet. The eardrops are of medium green, the bracelet of light green with apricot patches. *Colonel and Mrs. George Fong*

127. Jadeite bracelet at right is of a uniform green color; the one at left has patches of yellowish green. Chinese women usually have small hands and can wear these bracelets, which are only 3 inches in diameter; Western women cannot wear them unless they are cut and joined by links. (Beware of the recently imported jade bracelets, usually assembled from machine-cut sections with links, their prices should be lower.)

128. Bracelets of true jade with archaistic designs. The knowledgeable owner of Thi Antique Jade and Jewelry warns that many archaic-looking imported bracelets are actually made of green and brown serpentine.

rainbow. The bright green of jadeite was particularly treasured, and earned for it the name of "fei-ts'ai," meaning the shimmering feather of the kingfisher. This was a term used in the Sung dynasty (960–1279) and discarded; after the lapse of five hundred years, it was revived to honor the new jadeite. Words are lacking to describe the best of this "fei-ts'ai." It has been inadequately referred to as apple green, grass green, and leaf green by Western jewelers and collectors. It has also been compared to the green of the emerald, yet all emeralds pale beside the bright, vivid, vibrating green of jadeite.

Perhaps because it is impossible to describe a beautiful translucent green jadeite, the terms "imperial jade" and "imperial green" were haphazardly adopted. Since anything the Chinese considered valuable must necessarily be imperial, the terms "imperial jade" and "imperial green" have been much overused. When a dealer who is not familiar with jade shows you a stone with the slightest tinge of green, you are likely to be told that it is "imperial jade" or that the color is "imperial green."

Is there a standard by which a jade can be labeled "imperial"? This is a perfectly legitimate question in our "truth-in-packaging" age, and so we decided to put the question to many dealers and other persons interested in jade.

Among the most knowledgeable dealers, there seems to be a near-consensus—namely, that an "imperial jade" should, first of all, have the most brilliant green color; second, it should be extremely translucent; third, flawless; fourth, of uniform and pure color; fifth, of homogeneous texture. But there were small variations in the dealers' opinions, particularly in the order of importance of the various characteristics. One dealer said he never used the term because it really didn't mean anything.

From the less knowledgeable, we got all kinds of answers. Most of them said they had never thought of the question before, and, pressed for an answer, they protested, "You've got me there," or "I really can't say." Sometimes the answer took the form of a question: "Doesn't everybody use the term? So why ask me?" One person said with great confidence, "It means the piece belonged to the emperor what's-his-name—I mean Ch'ien-lung, of course."

Now let us consider a few things that may or may not have contributed to the adoption of the misleading terms. The expression "jade imperial" was created by Albert Jules Jacquemart, a French ceramic authority. However, he used it to refer to the bright green color on the imperial porcelains.

There is also a story—it cannot be substantiated—that once the emperor Ch'ien-lung was so impressed by the vivid green of jadeite that he decreed all good green jadeite should be brought to the palace for imperial use only. If he indeed issued such an order, it was totally disregarded, because all the lapidaries turned out green jadeite ornaments for sale, and people wore them as if no imperial order had ever been proclaimed. No ruling monarch would countenance such disobedience.

Of course, in China, yellow is the most esteemed of all colors. The Chinese consider themselves the descendants of the legendary Yellow Emperor (2698–2598 B.C.), who invented the compass and whose consort taught the people how to weave silk into material for garments. The Chinese call themselves the yellow race; and yellow was the color reserved for the emperor and his family, hence the term "imperial yellow." But imperial green? There has never been such an expression in the Chinese language. It reminds us of a noted writer on Chinese art who referred in one of his books to "The Chinese emperor on the peacock throne. . . ." A self-respecting Chinese emperor sat on a *dragon throne*, never on a peacock throne!

We feel it is to the interest of all concerned, dealers and buyers alike, to discontinue the loose and often indiscriminate use of the terms "imperial jade" and "imperial green."

Today jadeite has gained great popularity as the stone for jewelry.

Western designers use jadeite as the centerpiece and surround it with diamonds, although this practice does not necessarily enhance its beauty. Chinese taste still favors a deep, resonant green jadeite set in twenty-four carat (almost 100 percent pure) yellow gold. The contrast is breathtaking.

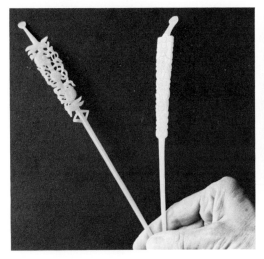

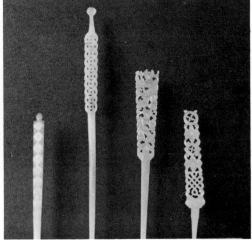

129. Hairpins of mutton-fat nephrite. Each is about 8 inches long and carved from a single piece of jade. At the top of each is the ear spoon—the Chinese did not consider it a breach of etiquette to remove ear wax with these spoons. *Dr. and Mrs. Marvin Hockabout*

130. Other jade hairpins. The tops of the two at right have broken off.

131. At center is a Mogul-style hairpin, inlaid with ruby, emerald, and green jadeite and goldstone. The other two pins have enameled silver ear spoons replacing the original jade.

132. The top of this hairpin is mutton-fat nephrite carved in the shape of a hand—truly a "head scratcher."

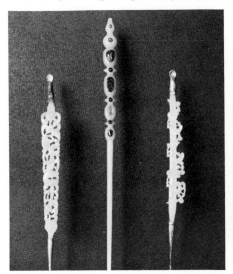

56

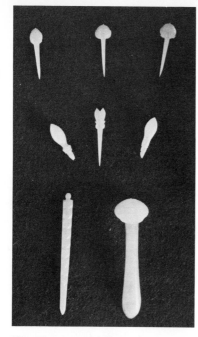

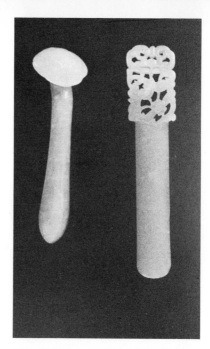

133. Hairpins of differing lengths and sizes for different purposes.

134. Hairpins used to anchor the hair knot.

The price of jewel jade has always been comparatively steady, but the market value of large specimens, like that of stocks, often undergoes wide fluctuations. In the early 1950s and even the 1960s, the price of carved jade objects was at an all-time low. People who started collecting during those years recall that they could pick up beautiful pieces of carved nephrite or jadeite for less than ten dollars. It was then that jade jewelers in the Far East, since raw Burmese jade was extremely difficult to get, began scrounging all over the Western world to find and buy large carved jade specimens, particularly those with good green color, that they could cut up for the choice jewel-quality parts, which they might make into things like ring cabochons. We have such a carved piece, a beautifully translucent but headless jadeite maiden of a light yellow (sometimes called onionskin yellow) color with a few patches of emerald green. The head, probably of a choice emerald green, had been neatly sawed off by someone who must have coveted it for another purpose. Our chance of finding raw material of similar color and transparency to use in making a replacement head was one in a thousand, and so eventually we made an

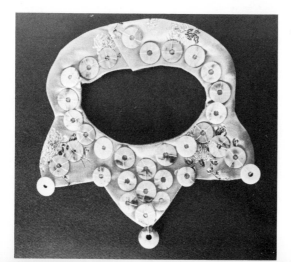

135. Small coin-type jadeite disks on a collar.

136. A necklace of carnelian and cloisonné beads. At center is a beautifully carved agate pendant showing a sailboat and boatman. The pendant is very like translucent light yellow jadeite. *Colonel and Mrs. George Fong*

137. Translucent jadeite pendant of mauve and green. *Colonel and Mrs. George Fong*

imitation jade head for the maiden—of glass and epoxy. After several attempts, we succeeded in producing a head that makes the maiden look passable—at least from a distance.

At a big West Coast antiques show several years ago, a dealer friend of ours had a carved butterfly of a uniform emerald green. When he proudly showed it to us, we noticed that the price was one thousand dollars—a bit on the high side then. At that point a man came up and asked to see the piece. After he had examined it carefully, he said, "I can cut six cabochons from this. If you'll give me the standard dealer's 20 percent discount, I'll take it."

Without replying, the dealer returned the butterfly to his showcase and deliberately turned the key with a loud click.

"Okay," said the would-be buyer, "I'll pay you the thousand."

"It is not for sale," said our dealer friend, turning his back.

The man left, angry and puzzled. Our friend was sputtering with rage. "I bought this from an old Chinese lady who was sick and needed money," he said. "When she gave me the butterfly, she was in tears. She begged me to sell it to someone who would cherish it—it had been in her family for generations!"

Even today magnificent jade pieces are still being destroyed by profit seekers. At the Sotheby Parke Bernet auction held in Hong Kong in December 1976, there were two magnificent Ch'ien-lung green jadeite screens (Ills. 203 and 204). *Arts of Asia* commented: "Several syndicates [were] formed during the viewing days with hopes of capturing the pair as raw material for new, smaller carvings, and more than one person was seen meticulously measuring them obviously with that thought in mind. . . . The screens were finally knocked down for $1.4 million to a private collector, who, it is hoped, will not chop them into jewelry."*

---

*H.K. $1.4 million, or approximately U.S. $300,000.

It is not uncommon today for a good stone for a ring to cost more than a thousand dollars. Green—a vibrant, vivid, bright, exciting green with a liquidlike translucency to bring out its depth, with no visible flaw, and without the slightest opaque whitish cloudiness or veins—leads in the price field. More recently, mauve or lavender has come into favor, although it still ranks below the good greens. The other colors—reddish brown (unless it is a true blood-red or tomato red, which is rare and occurs only in small flakes or patches), yellow, blue green, mixed colors, and the black—rank still lower and in that order.

It is difficult for an inexperienced person to judge a jade stone by itself, without comparing it with several others. When such a person wants to purchase a jewel jade, he is wise to go to a store specializing in jade. There he will be able to compare a number of stones in both color and price. If the price is what the purchaser wants to pay, and if the color of the stone pleases him, it will be the right jade for him.

Unfortunately, for both buyers and jewelers, many jewel stones can be altered or dyed to enhance their color, and jade—a relatively unstable stone—is one of them. Most reliable jade merchants do not want to have anything to do with dyed jade—they wish the term as well as the artificially colored stones would go away. Once in a long while, however, a dyed jade can slip in without the jeweler's even noticing it. How to deal with this problem is discussed in detail in Chapter 11, "An Investigation into Dyed Jade."

6

Jade–Our Common Language

Any collector of Chinese art objects is in some way a collector of jade. It can't be avoided. If you collect snuff bottles, you must have one or more bottles made from jade. And even if you are a snuff-bottle collector who happens to dislike jade, so that you avoid jade snuff bottles, you still must face the fact that almost 50 percent of the bottle stoppers are made of jade. Carved jade pieces, in fact, form the most important accessories of fine Chinese antiques. A Ming potiche, for example, may quite likely have lost its original lid, and have as a replacement a beautifully carved blackwood cover topped by a carved mutton-fat jade knob. And a lamp made from a Sung Lung-ch'ien vase is not fittingly elegant without a translucent green jadeite finial. To a connoisseur, this use of jade is not only correct but necessary.

Collectors of the above-mentioned categories of art objects are not, strictly speaking, jade collectors. A jade collector is one who is totally fascinated, entranced, and bewitched by the stone. He devotes all his time, energy, and money to the search for jade objects. We know a real estate agent who, when he sees a jade he wants, puts a down payment on it and, as soon as he has sold a house, pays off the balance from his commission so that he can take the jade home. The arrangement with his dealers worked all right for many years, until his wife complained: "When he sells a house, he doesn't even bring me a box of candy or a treat for the kids. He brings home another rock! Just look at the rocks all over the house—and every one cost a fortune!"

This lady is not exaggerating. A good piece of jade carving can cost a hundred thousand dollars—and that is really not an unreasonable price considering the fact that a beautifully carved jade, eight to twelve inches tall, takes a master carver at least half a year's time to create out of a piece of raw jade of the best quality. By contrast, a Sung celadon vase that was made to imitate jade would bring in half a million dollars now at the big auctions, but it would not have taken a potter two hours to shape it out of common clay, and not more than a week to fire it.

An experienced jade collector always goes to a dealer who specializes in jade, a dealer whose trade is 80 percent jade. He and his staff, if it is a big establishment, are of course experts. And if a collector has money and does not mind plunking down a few thousand dollars, he naturally goes to the most prestigious houses, such as Rare Art, Manheim, Edward Dominik's, or Gerald Dewey. A collector of lesser means can seek out dealers who offer smaller and less spectacular works at much more reasonable prices—say, between five hundred and a thousand dollars. These dealers are too numerous to mention. Inquire around and you will find several good and reliable ones in every city.

But what if you have only twenty-five to fifty dollars to spend, and you suddenly fall head over heels in love with jade, after having seen a piece owned by a friend? Do you have to deny yourself the pleasure of owning one or two pieces? No. Even with a small budget you can still be in the running as a collector of jade—small jade, to be sure. There are dealers to serve you and to take care of your needs at the small shops and even at the flea markets.

Don't belittle the flea market! Spending a day browsing at a flea market is the seventh most popular national pastime at present, and a well-managed, orderly market is a pleasure to both the sellers and buyers. People who want to sell only a few items do not need to get a business license or open a shop. For a few dollars a day in rent, anyone can secure space to sell whatever he wants to dispose of. Whereas a garage sale will attract only a few buyers, a flea market will attract hundreds (a really large one attracts thousands!). So a flea market is often the place to make great finds. For example, we know someone who was lucky enough to discover a peach bloom amphora for fifty cents. The owner had not liked it because of its splotchy glaze, and had given it a coat of bright orange paint, then decided to get rid of it. You can occasionally get jade pieces—rings, bracelets—at a fraction of their value. This is no secret to the regular browsers.

We are fortunate to be near such a market—one of the best-managed markets we have ever attended. It is held in a drive-in movie park, and the sellers are located in numbered spaces. A regular seller can have the same space as long as he wants it if he pays one month's rent in advance. Some even have cards printed: "Space R-7, Alameda Flea Market," for instance. The grounds are kept clean; and since dogs are not allowed, you never have to worry about putting your shoes into a smelly mess. There are at least ten security guards, walkie-talkie in hand, periodically circling the market. To our knowledge, no gun-point robberies have ever occurred, and fights are settled before they get out of hand. Strayed children or lost items are immediately announced over a loudspeaker system. The refreshment stand offers good and prompt service. Many people pay the twenty-five cents admission and come in just for the fun of it, or for the exercise of walking the nearly two miles of lanes and meeting and talking with their friends.

Such a big market naturally has specialized dealers. At this one at least eight sell nothing except jades and other precious and semiprecious stones, but our favorite dealer is Mrs. Palmer. She has an agent who goes regularly to Hong Kong and also attends the Canton Fair. Every four to six weeks she receives a package from him. Sometimes it contains intricately carved jade flowers; other times it will contain amber, malachite, silver rings, necklaces, and similar things—no monumental pieces, of course, but everything of the best workmanship. Many of the items may be slightly damaged, but they can be sanded down and polished to look like perfect pieces. You can do the work yourself with various grades of sandpaper that are available at rock shops. These are antique pieces that the Chinese government accumulated through the people's "donations." "No new junks," Mrs. Palmer points out; that is the way she refers to the new machine-carved pieces that flood the market today.

Mrs. Palmer, a woman in her seventies, has been selling at this market for the last fifteen years—she almost never misses a weekend. In the course of those fifteen years, she has sold many beautiful things at moderate prices.

Mrs. Palmer has style. She arrives at the market with a big showcase with folding legs, crammed full of beautiful and eye-catching things, and with three chairs: a director's chair for herself, and two folding camp stools for her customers. She is the only seller whose customers sit down before and while doing business. That's the proper way, she believes, and she does things properly. She also believes in treating people fairly. In a flea market, dickering and haggling are often a way of life, but not with her. She is an institution—you don't dicker with her any more than you would with the IRS.

By midday, after she has greeted all her friends and customers with "Come back to see me later. I have something to show you," she reminds herself it is time to take a walk to improve her circulation. Seeing a familiar face, she beckons and says, "Will you sit here a minute while I walk around a little bit? If anybody wants me, just say I'll be back soon." Then off she goes. Many sellers and buyers have been seen "baby-sitting" for Mrs. Palmer.

She's adept at putting people down if they deserve it. One woman had been telling her for weeks about a jade ring she wanted to sell to her, describing how beautiful the green was, and the fine setting of 100-

percent Chinese gold with the Chinese shop mark on the inside. Finally Mrs. Palmer said, "Don't keep telling me about it—bring it and let me see it." When the woman at last produced the ring, which was rather commonplace, Mrs. Palmer asked quietly, "Is this the ring that you have been telling me about for all these weeks?"—and handed it back without another word.

Another time a man brought in a jade piece to sell to her. She commented that the asking price was too high. "But," protested the man, "Mrs. Palmer said it was worth that much."

"Oh, do you know Mrs. Palmer?" She looked at him steadily for a minute. "Say hello to her for me when you see her again." She handed the jade back. "Just a minute—here's my business card, with my name in both English and Chinese."

Once we were stopped by a middle-aged woman.

"Are you Mr. Chu?"

"Yes."

"I have brought something to show you."

She carefully unwrapped a package and produced a necklace consisting of twelve white jadeite beads with some drab green spots on them, three rose quartz beads, and a jadeite pendant, white with streaks of green, carved into a double gourd with a broken leaf attached.

"I have already had it appraised. Here." She handed over a sheet of paper.

Indeed, it was a signed appraisal from the owner of a "gallery" specializing in "Asian treasures." It explained that the necklace was that of a high-ranking mandarin and consisted of twelve jade and three pink beads. (Apparently the appraiser did not know that they were rose quartz.) It said further that the jade gourd is a symbol of good luck and therefore very valuable. Market value as of the date of appraisal: five thousand dollars.

"Isn't it a beautiful necklace, Mr. Chu?"

"It's okay."

"Do you think the price is right?"

"Certainly not."

"How much do you think it is worth?"

"Frankly, I don't know. I am not an appraiser."

"Do you think anybody here can tell me how much it is really worth?"

"Well, maybe Mrs. Palmer can." I thought Mrs. Palmer could certainly put this woman in her place and do it in the proper way.

"You mean the black lady with a lot of jade in her showcase?"

"Exactly."

Half an hour later we passed Mrs. Palmer's place.

"Mr. Chu, Mr. Chu!" she exclaimed. "I just saw a necklace appraised at five thousand dollars! I wish you could see it!"

"I did see it, Mrs. Palmer."

"Isn't that terrible?" She was huffing and puffing with outrage. "Five thousand dollars!"

"Well, I'm sorry."

"Why are you sorry, Mr. Chu?"

"Because you're so upset."

"I'm more than 'upset' at the nerve and ignorance of some people."

Some of her friends, for whom "flea-marketeering" is not exactly a life-style, come to see and talk with her and, while doing so, to pick up one or two of the good old jade pieces she has just received from Hong Kong. There is her dentist friend, and there is her banker, a Chinese gentleman who is an avid jade collector. When she and her banker meet, the conversation verges on a contest in connoisseurship:

"This carving doesn't do anything for the stone."

"Oh, yes, it does! Just look at it this way—"

Many of her customers are young Chinese—girls buying their first jade, or boys buying presents for their betrothed. They want something with the heirloom look, not brand-new machine-cut objects from Hong Kong.

Mrs. Palmer lives in Oakland's Chinatown, where 90 percent of her neighbors are Chinese, and most of them speak little English. She speaks no Chinese, but she says there is no problem of communication. "You show the Chinese a piece of jade," she explains, "and at once their eyes light up. Then they smile. Then you become their friend, and you understand one another. Jade is our common language."

PART II
Practical Information

7
Physical Properties of Jade

After having said how beautiful, how noble, how divine, and how important to the Chinese culture jade is, we must now turn our backs on aesthetic matters and examine the physical aspects of nephrite and jadeite as stones or minerals, and consider what their superior qualities, if any, are. Although it is proverbially foolish to tear off the petals of a flower to find where its beauty lies — and how devoid of pleasure that process is — it is necessary to examine some basic scientific facts concerning jade, for it is this basic knowledge that will enable the beginning collector to differentiate jade from the various kinds of pseudojade as well as from man-made imitations.

The jade material used by the Chinese for carving was of two main varieties. The chemical formula of nephrite is $Ca(Mg,Fe)_3(SiO_3)_4$; basically, it is a *silicate of calcium and magnesium.* The chemical formula for jadeite is $NaAlSi_2O_6$; basically, it is a *silicate of sodium and aluminum.* These minerals, exclusively, are the "jade" that the Chinese called Yü. A third kind, chloromelanite, a dark green to green black to black stone often considered a variety of jadeite, is rarely found in color attractive enough for carving. (The cabbage shown in Ill. 26 is an exception.)

From the above chemical formulas, it is clear that nephrite and jadeite are two different minerals. However, they have many similarities:

138. Jade boulders or blocks are first cut into slabs.

139. A jade slab. Note that the fractures (also termed "veins") are always splintery and never conchoidal.

1. One is just about as hard as the other. (Of this quality, we will say more later on.)
2. Both are very tough, nephrite being the tougher of the two. Neither is very easy to break.
3. Their fractures, if any, are always splintery and never conchoidal—that is, like the pattern in a broken shell, or chipped glass or porcelain.
4. In their pure state, both nephrite and jadeite are white, but impurities give them the full range of colors.

From ancient times to the eighteenth century, all the Chinese jade artifacts were made from nephrite, most of the material coming from Chinese Turkestan. During Emperor Ch'ien-lung's time the area was formally, by military conquest, annexed to the Chinese empire. Since then it has been known as Singkiang, which means, literally, "New Territory." Except during ancient times, when China may have produced a small quantity of jade (it soon became exhausted), most Chinese jade objects were carved from Sinkiang nephrite, which is of superior quality. It has few inclusions and is uniformly hard: it cannot be scratched by the blade of a pocketknife. A collector of some experience will usually be able to tell Sinkiang nephrite from the nephrite of other parts of the world. (This is further explained in the chapter, "Jade Throughout the World.") Nephrite from Sinkiang was known as "true jade."* Occasionally, since the eighteenth century, a uniformly green nephrite with black specks from Siberia has also been used.

---

*As mentioned in the chapter, "Jade for Jewelry," when jadeite was first discovered during the Ming dynasty it was not accepted by the Chinese, and a law was soon made prohibiting the selling of the newly discovered material as true jade. How strictly the law was enforced is not known.

However, people soon found that jadeite has many qualities superior to those of nephrite. Although to the purists mutton-fat nephrite (its unctuous, soft whiteness calls to mind the congealed fat of mutton) perhaps cannot be surpassed, green nephrite in all its various shades can never compare with the exciting apple or emerald green of jadeite. Furthermore, jadeite has a brilliant luster, the ability to reflect light like a mirror when it is polished to a high gloss. Nephrite, on the other hand—with the exception of special types such as the black nephrite of Wyoming—will merely take on a waxy look when polished. Even though some collectors of antique jades still profess a preference for the waxy and intimate feeling of nephrite, nearly 99 percent of the expensive jewel jade today is jadeite because of its brilliant luster and hardness.

Hardness

Friedrich Mohs (1773–1839), a German mineralogist, devised a scale (the Mohs Scale) to measure the hardness of gemstones and minerals. On a scale of ten, he selected ten minerals as representative:

1.	Talc	6.	Feldspar
2.	Gypsum	7.	Quartz
3.	Calcite	8.	Topaz
4.	Fluorspar	9.	Corundum
5.	Apatite	10.	Diamond

Any mineral on this list can *be* scratched by the one with the next higher number, and can scratch the one with the number just preceding.

Any unlisted mineral that is as hard as one appearing on the list naturally will rate the same hardness number on the scale. Nephrite is rated as 6 to 6½ (some mineralogists say only 5¾ to 6) and jadeite as 6½ to 7.

This information is important because it gives the jade collector the first important tool, but certainly not the only one, to determine whether a mineral is jade or some substance that is softer than jade, notably soapstone, serpentine, and/or bowenite, which is a more compact form of serpentine.

The test is very simple. Nephrite has a hardness of 6 and jadeite is even harder; neither one should be scratched by the steel blade of a pocketknife. Please note that we say the steel blade of a *pocketknife.* A steel file or any tool made for industrial use will definitely scratch nephrite, but not jadeite.

To make the test, do not pass the knife blade ritualistically over the stone. Select a place, preferably quite smoothly polished—for instance, under the foot of a piece—so that if the knife can and does scratch the stone, its appearance will not be ruined. Press the blade firmly upon the stone and draw it a distance of at least one-fourth of an inch. When you can see a definite mark, you have made a successful test; you do not need to repeat it—you need only to observe the result. Note particularly the direction to "press firmly," rather than "press hard." Several years ago, during one of our lectures, we were asked how to determine whether a stone is jade or a substitute. We explained that the first step is to eliminate the possibility of a softer material, by making the scratch test, and unfortunately we used the phrase "press hard." When the questioner got home, she repeated our directions to her husband, who immediately decided to test her beautiful ring, a large cabochon of black Wyoming jade. He scratched it once, and did not see a white line or a black one (it is difficult to see a black line on a black jade), so he pressed harder, and still harder. Being a six-foot-two athlete who played tennis every week, the husband had a good deal of strength and perseverance.

The next day, the bewildered lady phoned us. "We made the test," she said. "We tried many times, but we still don't know whether it is jade or not."

"What color is the line—black or white?"

"There is no line—there's a groove."

We met with her to see the test results. Sure enough, her husband had pressed the knife so hard that he had made a distinct groove on the surface of the jade, although it was barely visible without a magnifier. The stone had to be resurfaced—lightly sanded and repolished—in order to remove the groove.

If you have made the test correctly, and if the mark looks white, it means that the knife has scratched the stone, and you can be sure that the stone is not jade. It could be serpentine, often nicknamed Soochow jade, or bowenite, also called Soochow jade, or it might be Korean jade (as explained in Chapter 10).* If the mark is black, or steely, the stone has scratched the steel blade. The stone may very well be jade, but not necessarily so, because there are other stones that are as hard as jade and superficially look like jade. Other tests must be made, especially if the jade object is a very expensive one.

It can be stated here that almost any stone softer than jade is invariably cheaper than jade, and can be said to be inferior to jade. Therefore, a scratch test is absolutely necessary. Never trust your eyes alone. Of course eyesight has many useful functions in relation to minerals and gemstones, such as judging the color and purity and detecting flaws. But the eyes cannot tell you the hardness of the stone.

In applying the scratch test, keep the following things in mind:

1. Archaic Chinese jades, particularly those that have been buried for a long time, will have been altered or calcified by chemicals in the earth. They will have developed a softer "skin," which can be scratched. Therefore, a scratch test *should not* be applied to a piece of valuable archaic jade.

2. Nephrite that has been through a fire will have lost its color and glossiness and will have turned chalky white, with shiny spots. The Chinese call it "chicken-bone jade," and they value it because the pieces

---

*"New jade" is the term used in the Far East.

are usually very old. (However, many nephrite objects of low-quality jade were deliberately burned to create fake archaic pieces. The Chinese scornfully refer to them as "fritters.") Pieces of chicken-bone jade are naturally softer, and can be scratched. At high temperatures jadeite will fuse like liquid glass, so it is of no concern here.

3. Chinese lapidaries usually rub a coat of hard wax over their products to hide the unpolished places and give a better overall look. This wax can last for many years, particularly if the jade piece has not been handled very much. Therefore, a scratch may be just on the wax coating. It is always advisable to wipe a stone very thoroughly first, before you make the scratch test.

4. Ideally, the surface to be tested should be smooth and well polished. If you have to make a test on a rough surface, there may be a black line (indicating that the stone has scratched the steel blade) and a disconnected white line as well. This can mean that, because of the rough surface, some jade particles have been pulled off the surface by the blade. There is no reason to discredit the stone if a clear and distinct black line does show.

Both nephrite and jadeite are hard stones, but they are, particularly nephrite, really not hard enough. A good gemstone has to be at least as hard as quartz (H-7) or, better still, harder. The reason (as mentioned in Chapter 5) is that dust is full of tiny particles of quartz, and a stone softer than quartz will not wear well. Jadeite can make the grade, but nephrite is slightly below the standard.

Along with hardness, another important quality demands consideration: the toughness of the stone. Here we can use glass and plexiglass for an analogy. A piece of glass can scratch a piece of plexiglass easily, and so we say that glass is harder than plexiglass. Yet if we drop the glass, it immediately breaks into pieces. But we can drop the plexiglass over and over again, and it will never break. So we say plexiglass is tougher than glass.

Nephrite has this superior quality of toughness. Fifty tons of pressure are required to crush a 1" x 1" x 1" cube of nephrite. It is the second toughest mineral in the world, next to the black diamond. Since black diamonds can be used only for industrial purposes, we can say nephrite is the toughest gemstone in the world. Jadeite is also very tough, though less so than nephrite.

This quality is what makes jade so endearing to a Chinese, who derives great pleasure in having a small carved jade to hang on his belt or to keep in his pocket to fondle. Naturally, in such usage a jade may be dropped quite often, but it will not break or shatter. It is also because of this quality of toughness that jade, particularly nephrite, can be cut very thin and carved into intricate pierced patterns.

Jade is, therefore, seemingly indestructible—many of the items on the market today are actually over a hundred years or even several hundred years old. Their toughness is essentially due to their structure: Nephrite is formed by interlocking microscopic fibers, jadeite by fibers and interlock-

140. A drawing showing the fibrous structure of a magnified piece of nephrite.

141. The interlocking crystals of jadeite (a drawing).

ing tiny crystals. Unlike minerals that show distinct crystalline formations, they have no cleavages to weaken their structure.

However, this toughness presents great difficulty to prospectors and people who make their living quarrying jade. The standard advice (or joke) relayed to novice prospectors is: "If you find a jade boulder too heavy to lift, don't swing your hammer at it—the hammer may bounce back and crack your head." The traditional method of breaking up a large formation into manageable size was to build fires on the stone in the late evening. When the surface was very hot, the fires were extinguished. The cold night air then caused the boulder to cool so rapidly that it would crack, and thus be easier to break up. This method was not only wasteful; it also made fissures appear in the stone. The modern method is to cut the jade formation into convenient sizes on the spot, using diamond saws. This method cuts down waste tremendously.

Specific Gravity

The next thing to consider is specific gravity. We have often heard the comment: "It's very heavy, so it must be jade."

Many stones are heavy, but that does not make them jade. However, patently, some substances *are* heavier than others—and heavier, or less heavy, in comparison with any material one chooses as a standard. The material commonly used as a standard is water. (One cubic centimeter of distilled water at 4°C weighs exactly one gram.) The ratio between any tested material and an equal volume of water is called its specific gravity.

The specific gravity of nephrite is 3.0 (2.90 to 3.20). This means that nephrite is three times heavier than water. The specific gravity of jadeite is 3.3 (3.20 to 3.40), so jadeite is 3.3 times heavier than water. Each different mineral has its own specific gravity; therefore specific gravity can be a useful means of identification.

There are many ways to measure specific gravity. The simplest is to submerge the stone in water. Weigh both the stone and the water displaced by the stone, and then divide the weight of the stone by the weight of the displaced water. The result will represent the specific gravity of the stone.

An easier and more accurate way to find the specific gravity of a stone is to purchase certain heavy liquids that come in bottles, each with the specific gravity marked on the bottle. Drop your stone successively into the various bottled liquids until—in one bottle—it neither sinks nor floats but remains suspended and stationary. The specific gravity marked on that particular bottle will be the specific gravity of the stone.

This method of identification is not so easy as the scratch test, which eliminates only the softer substitutes. However, if your jade is costly, it is worthwhile to have it thoroughly tested. A good laboratory or a well-equipped jewelry store will do it for you for a fee.

Index of Refraction

When light enters from one medium into another of a different density, it bends. For example, if you stand above or beside a swimming pool and look at swimmers standing in the pool, you will notice that their arms or bodies seem broken at the point where air and water meet. The light coming to your eyes through the air is normal, but the light traveling through the water has been bent. This phenomenon is called refraction. Almost every stone has a different angle of refraction. The index of refraction, a constant, is derived from this angle of refraction.

Besides serving as another good means of identifying a mineral or stone, the effect of refraction contributes greatly to the beauty of a stone, particularly the transparent kind. The diamond is a good example. To use this effect to the best advantage, a diamond has to be faceted in such a way that, when the light enters it, the light is bent and then dispersed by a prism effect into rainbow colors. These refracted and dispersed light beams hit the different facets and are reflected back into our eyes with a dazzling effect.

In the case of jade, both nephrite and jadeite, the effect created by this phenomenon is not significant. But their indices of refraction provide another means of identification, one that jewelers use. The index of refraction for nephrite is 1.60 to 1.63; for jadeite, 1.65 to 1.68.

Chemical Analysis

The chemical formulas of both nephrite and jadeite were explained earlier. The chemical analysis of a stone will give unmistakable proof of its identity, but such an analysis should be made by a professional mineralogist working in a laboratory, preferably one specializing in identifying jade. However, such an analysis should be considered only as a court of last resort; in most cases, it is not necessary to go this far to arrive at a conclusive judgment.

8

A Master Jade Carver
at Work

Hong Kong is deservedly called the jade capital of the world. Here, fabulous antique jade, of both the monumental and the small exquisite kinds, is brought from all over the world to be auctioned off to connoisseurs and knowledgeable dealers, wealthy collectors, and their agents. Great quantities of new jade objects are produced by workshops, large and small, to answer the increasing demands of newly converted jade fanciers.

Because of its strategic location, Hong Kong's position is unique. Geographically it is close to the source of the world's finest raw jade, the unsurpassable Burmese jadeite. Although the famed nephrite from Khotan and Yarkand is still unavailable, there is the less expensive Taiwan jade, and also the newly developed nephrite from British Columbia and other parts of the world, which arrives daily by boat and air. And Hong Kong now has a number of good carvers; their techniques are second to none in the world, and their workshops have incorporated new machinery that saves time and waste. Jade work demands the meticulous care and patience that only oriental people seem to have, and many young Chinese, because of the increasing demand for jade and the relatively good pay, are willing to be apprenticed to the trade. This was particularly so when jade prices rose 600 percent in 1973. More workshops were established, and they were humming with ceaseless activity. As a result, there was an oversupply of jade objects. Prices dropped, but not extensively—not enough to demote jade as a viable product.

Actually, there is never an oversupply of *great* jades. These not only have to be made from the best raw jade, but also must be created by the hands of master carvers—and the number of such craftsmen is never large. After all, jade rings, jade bracelets, beads for necklaces, the pendants of hearts and disks, are now done partly by machine; but what of the grasshopper sitting like a live one on a head of cabbage? Or a statue of the goddess of mercy, her face filled with compassion for suffering mankind? The face of the statue may be a delicate lavender, her robe the glistening white of purity, and the background a bamboo grove of lush green and tender yellow. Nothing but human hands can create such art, and a jade masterpiece like one of these cannot be completed in less than six months.

Among the masters of creative jade art, Mr. Chu Man-chi stands at the forefront. Mr. Chu is not related to the authors, although we came from an area around Shanghai and have the same surname. (In China when two persons who have the same surname meet, the customary greeting is, "Five hundred years ago we were in the same family.") It is regrettable that we have not had the chance to interview this jade artist ourselves. Our portrait of him relies entirely upon an *Arts of Asia* article, "Chu's" (November–December 1974).*

142. Master carver Mr. Chu Man-chi at work.

Mr. Chu served his apprenticeship in Shanghai. He was so dedicated to his art that he became proficient with both large specimens and small delicate items, a rare versatility, since most carvers specialize in one type only. His move to Hong Kong took place early in the postwar years —oddly, because of the misfortune of a friend, a Mr. Ma, a rich jade merchant. Ma had bid on and bought an expensive jadeite boulder. When this was sawed open, it proved to be of only ordinary quality, not good enough to be cut into jewel stones. The carvers in Hong Kong at that time

*The pictures in this chapter were taken by Mr. Stephen Markbreiter, and are reproduced by permission and through the courtesy of *Arts of Asia*.

could not carve anything but cabochons, and so, in order to recoup his loss, Ma asked Chu to come to Hong Kong, hoping that Chu's versatility would enable him to make better use of the jade and turn it into figurines and other desirable objects.

Chu used his skill and ingenuity to turn his friend's mistake into a profitable venture, but Ma thereafter proceeded to make more bad buys and eventually lost all his money. Bidding on jade boulders is a risky business—you cannot see what is inside the rough, brownish skin of the stone, although a small patch (called a window) less than a square inch in area and a quarter-inch deep is often cut away and polished so that prospective buyers can examine the stone and make their estimates as to the probable colors and eventual value.

143. Third son Jonas Chu demonstrates the old-fashioned treadle lathe.

144. A worker at the treadle lathe (from *Investigations and Studies in Jade* (New York: privately printed, 1906). *The Bishop Collection*

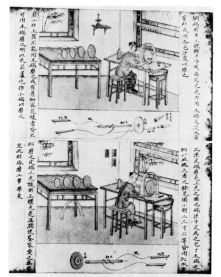

At this point, perhaps, it should be explained that the term "carving jade" or "jade carving" is a misnomer, since no metal can cut a piece of jade. Actually, "jade carving" refers to the process of grinding away the unwanted portion of the stone until what you want emerges, and then polishing it until it shines in splendor. To achieve this, a loose grit mixed with water is used on a turning lathe powered by a foot pedal. Nowadays, the grit of natural stones has been replaced by man-made Carborundum, which has a hardness of 9, and the lathe is driven by a motor at a slow speed. After the rough shape has been achieved using a coarse grit, the carver refines his work with a medium grit, then a fine grit. The grit can be loosely classified as coarse (100–200), medium (200–300), and fine (400–600). When the carver is satisfied with his work, he starts the polishing and continues it until the product becomes translucent and glossy and the colors show to the best advantage. To do the polishing, a material softer than jade is used. In the old times, perhaps it was the skin of a dry gourd; now, a polishing powder such as tin oxide is preferred.

Actually, the process of carving has not changed much from the old days. The one and only important tool is the lathe, whether driven by a motor or a foot pedal. The various attachments and drills can be made by the carver himself, using soft metal such as the iron that ordinary nails are made of. Soft iron works better than hard steel because soft metal can hold the grit just a split second longer and therefore get more grinding done.

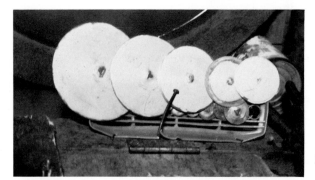

145. Cutting disks.

146. A complete array of carving tools.

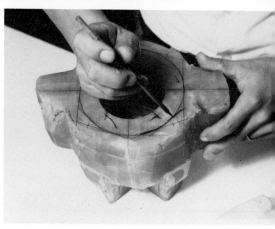

147. These carvers make all their own tools out of iron.

148. The designer outlines the next area to be cut away.

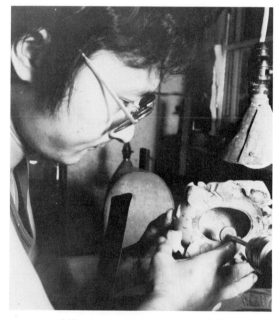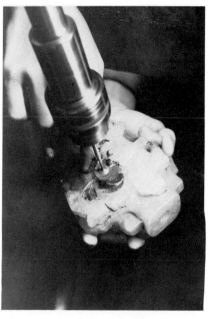

149. A carver using a cutting disk.

150. A cutting disk used with Carborundum, an abrasive.

151. A small disk is used for detailed work.

152. In the bowls beneath the carver's hands are three grades of Carborundum.

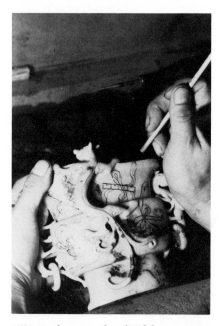 

153. As the inner details of the stone are revealed, the carver often must suspend his work to alter the design.

154. The carver also modifies the design of this figure.

Chu opened his own workshop after the failure of his friend. He had five sons attending school in Shanghai, and he brought them to Hong Kong to learn the trade. A perfectionist himself, he insisted that his sons learn from the bottom up because he believes that one must acquire all the necessary skills before he can supervise others.

In China, there is a saying that no one knows a boy better than his own father. Perhaps the saying is equally true if reversed. At any rate, Chu's sons are reported as saying, in the *Arts of Asia* interview: "Our father is a first-class artist but no businessman. Whatever he carves has to be perfect, whether the material is expensive or cheap. His integrity is such that he feels obliged to point out to another carver, even from a different workshop, what he thinks is wrong about a particular example of carving, sometimes hurting the other man's feelings unnecessarily."

However, in his own workshop (called "Chu's," located on Kimberley Street, Kowloon), he works every day at his lathe among his thirty employees, a picture of dedication and smiling contentment.

Above
1. The famous Jade Pagoda (see Chapter 3 for details). *Oakland Museum*

Left
2. Tiger of chicken-bone jade. The suggestion that it might represent an alligator instead is negated by the appearance of the tail. Chou dynasty. *Chingwah Lee Collection*

3. *Ya-chang*—symbol of rank, probably for a marshal. The hole is conical, characteristic of earlier jades. Chou dynasty. *Chingwah Lee Collection*

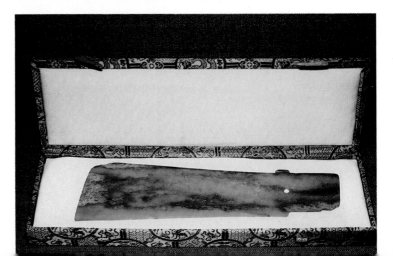

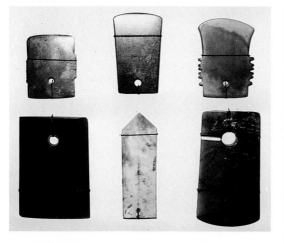

Top left
4. Scrapers and axe blades, probably ceremonial. Chou dynasty. *Chingwah Lee Collection*

Top right
5. A jade fish, eroded in spots. Mythology has it that when the carp succeeded in leaping the rapids, it turned into a dragon. Diameter, 5". Probably Han dynasty. *Chingwah Lee Collection*

Left
6. Rhyton with split-tail dragons; one stands on the elephant. Sung dynasty. Height, 7". *Chingwah Lee Collection*

Below
7. Ceremonial vessel, eighteenth-century reproduction of Chou dynasty style. *Chingwah Lee Collection*

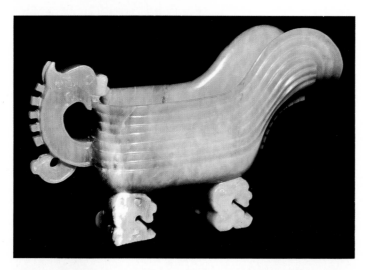

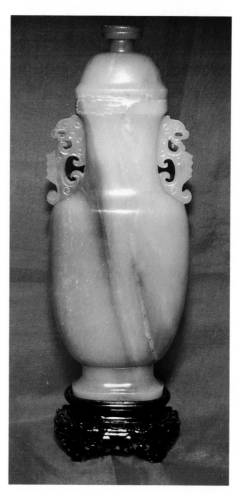

Right
8. Urn of rare yellow nephrite in archaic bronze form. Height, 12″. *Chingwah Lee Collection*

Below
9. Jadeite brush washer. The carver took advantage of the brown color to form the lotus leaves, the flower, and the dragonfly. The wood stand fits over the bottom, concealing the stem that completes the plant. Diameter, 4″. Ch'ien-lung. *Chingwah Lee Collection*

10. Insects feeding on a melon patch. Diameter, 9″. Late K'ang-hsi. *Chingwah Lee Collection*

11. Snuff bottle. The skin of the stone was used effectively to form the hydra decoration. *Chingwah Lee Collection*

12. Pebble-shaped red jadeite snuff bottle. *Chingwah Lee Collection*

13. Emerald green jade brooch. Contemporary. *Chingwah Lee Collection*

14. *Hsün chi*, astronomical instrument. Chou period. *Chingwah Lee Collection*

15. Roosters and plant made by master carver Chu Man-chi in 1974. *Photograph by Stephen Markbreiter; courtesy of* Arts of Asia

16. Jade censer from the Summer Palace, of uniform green with yellow magnolia flowers on top. Gilding is original. Height, approx. 22″. Ming or Early Ch'ing period. *Foster Collection*

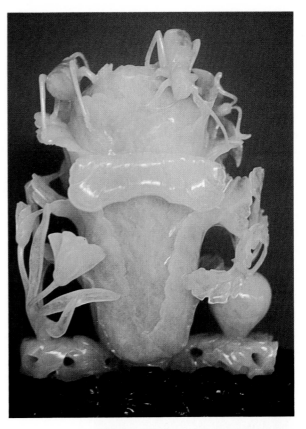

17. Jadeite cabbage vase. *Foster Collection*

18. Jadeite ewer photographed against a Pacific Ocean sunset. *Foster Collection*

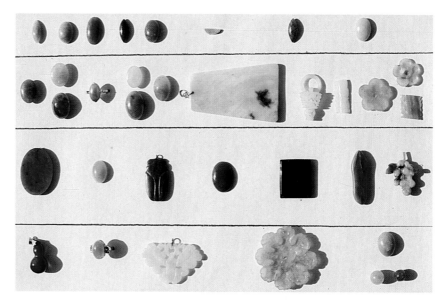

19. *Top row, left to right:* Group of five dyed Burmese jadeite cabochons; a cross section; dyed piece after eight months in sunlight; piece after boiling in oil. *Second row:* Six Burmese jadeite cabochons; an emerald green ring; piece of Burmese jadeite shaped and polished by the authors; examples of Sinkiang nephrite. *Third row:* Nephrite from Taiwan, Siberia, Alaska, British Columbia, Wyoming, California, and a botryoidal grape cluster. *Fourth row:* Pseudojades—carnelian (red jade), chrysoprase (Australian jade), bowenite (Korean jade), serpentine (new jade or Soochow jade), and aventurine (Indian jade).

20. *Top row, left to right:* Pieces carved by the authors—rose quartz peach with fluorite leaves; hyacinth bulb, made from an amethyst pebble, with Taiwan jade leaf and ivory roots; amber snuff bottle in shape of Buddha's-hand citron; jadeite peach; screen with coral fish; lapis brush rest shaped like a mountain; jadeite gourd; California jadeite knife. *Bottom row:* bowenite elephant; turquoise baby boy; Bodhidharma in smoky quartz; malachite boy riding the waves; carnelian dog; Taiwan jade ram.

9

How to Carve Your Own Jade

If you are a serious collector of jade, or want to be one, there is no better way to derive more appreciation and understanding of your collection, or to enhance your pride in possessing it, than to make a few jade objects of your own. Needless to say, it is also the quickest way to educate yourself so that you learn to distinguish genuine jade from pseudojades and man-made imitations.

All this sounds like a big order, but actually it is not. The ancients created jade objects with practically their bare hands. You can do the same, but in a much easier way.

First, visit gem and rock shows. There are always trimmings for sale at a few dollars apiece. These were cut away by a lapidary specializing in certain kinds of carvings—cabochons, bracelets, figurines, and so on. Often they are available in surprisingly interesting colors. Usually they are in the form of slabs and oddly shaped pieces, except for the rounds cut from the inside of bracelets (see Ill. 155). Use your imagination in choosing them, and look for their potential. Some of them may already resemble a simple human or animal form, a bamboo trunk, a knife, a certain fruit. Perhaps the seller failed to see this, or did not care to do the work even if he saw the possibilities. In any case, you do not have to bid on a boulder and saw it apart!

Put your raw jade on the table and visualize what you want to do. With a pencil sketch the object you want to make, directly on the jade itself. If

155. Jade cutouts like these are available from bracelet carvers at very reasonable prices. They can be sanded and polished for use as paperweights, or you can choose one and do some simple carving.

you have several choices in mind, wipe the first sketch off and try another, and still another. Estimate how much jade you will have to get rid of before your intended object emerges. As we have already said, carving jade is nothing but slowly grinding away the unwanted portion, and then polishing what is left to the degree of glossiness you want. Therefore, the less you have to grind off, the less time and work for you.

After you have determined what you want to do, sketch the object clearly on the jade. Then go to a rock shop and buy several grades of sandpaper: 1) coarse grade (around 100), 2) medium grade (around 200), 3) fine grade (400), and 4) prepolish (600). Also buy polishing powder (tin oxide or some other polishing agent). These sandpapers are not the ordinary flint paper. They are coated with Carborundum or other equally hard grit, and are waterproof. As to how many sheets of paper you will need, consult the rock-shop proprietor.

156. Let's make a peach from a mauve-colored piece of jadeite less than ¼ inch thick. It is easier to shape the piece with a whetstone made of any kind of abrasive harder than the jadeite (H-7+) and of a grit of about 120.

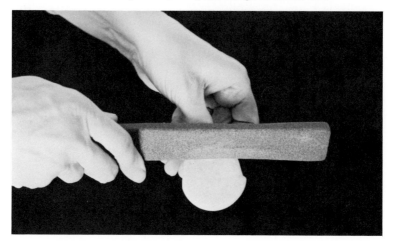

Above left:
157. Be patient. It will take more than six hours to carve a round block into the rough shape of a peach like this.

Above right:
158. Now we can refine the shape a bit. Draw a black line along the middle, and work back and forth along the line with the sharp edge of the whetstone until you get a groove.

Right:
159. Switch to sandpaper (see instructions in text). Sand and polish the entire piece, including the edges of the groove. When finished (after ten to fifteen hours), you will have a jade peach like this one. The authors made the stand from broken pieces of blackwood Chinese furniture that they save for this purpose.

First, use the coarse grade of paper to shape the stone (preferably putting water on the paper and keeping it wet). When you are through with this step, your object should have assumed its rough shape. This coarsest grade of paper will remove the unwanted part faster, but it will also leave very deep scratches.

Now change to the medium-grit paper—and remember one important thing: Wash the jade again and again, until you are sure that not one particle of coarse grit is being carried over; even one particle will create trouble for you by continuing to make deep scratches on the jade. The medium-grit paper will further refine the shape of the object, and also reduce the deep scratches into shallower ones.

Again, wash the jade thoroughly as you change to the fine-grade paper. The object at this stage is to smooth out the surface; the shape will not change noticeably. After you are through, the surface will be smooth and will have acquired a slight sheen.

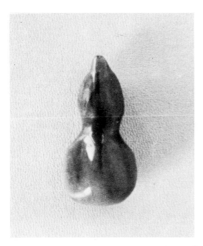

160. A roughly wedge-shaped slice of jadeite of an intriguing olive green and yellow color cost the authors seventy-five cents at one time. It could have been carved into a very realistic slice of pickle. Here, however, with a little more work, it has become a double gourd (see Color Plate 20).

161. This piece of jadeite suggested a section of bamboo even when it was rough, so there was no need to deliberate over what to make out of it. The jade is set in a blackwood screen with a bamboo motif (this screen too was made from a piece of broken furniture).

Wash the jade thoroughly once more before changing to the 600 paper. After you are through using this finest paper, the jade will look more translucent and its color will seem to have been enhanced. It should also have a silken sheen.

You can stop at this point, but it's a shame not to continue your effort until your creation is as fine as you can make it, and that's where polishing comes in. The difference between sanding and polishing is that in sanding you use grit harder than jade, but polishing is done with powder softer than jade. In the old Chinese workshops, as mentioned earlier, they used dried gourd skin; now, however, we have several kinds of powder available to us. An advanced amateur carver may prefer some other substance, but tin oxide seems to be a good all-around material to use, particularly for the beginner. It will not leave any stain in invisible cracks or fissures.

Make a paste with the polishing powder and water. Spread this on a piece of clean (free from grit, sand, or dust) canvas or leather (we think leather is better). Rub the stone on it, adding drops of water to the leather to keep it wet. Continue polishing until the jade develops a high luster.

How long will it take to make a simple design from, say, a two-inch by two-inch by one-half-inch piece of jade? About thirty hours, to do a good job; twenty hours, to do a so-so job. The time will be divided about equally among the various steps of the process. Jadeite takes a little more time, nephrite a little less.

If you are making a three-dimensional object, a whetstone stick made of synthetic hard grit will do the shaping more easily and better (Ill. 156). The result will certainly be worth the time and elbow grease.

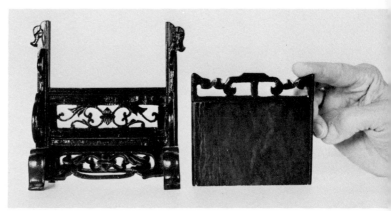

162. We decided to assemble a jade screen and stand. First we found this stand.

163. Next, we found a piece of Canadian nephrite, a beautiful deep green in color, about 3¾ inches by 4¾ inches in size—slightly smaller than the stand. After shaping, sanding, and polishing the jade, we glued a blackwood edging to both sides of it so that it would fit inside the grooves on the stand uprights. Then we fitted the upper edge of the jade with a fancy wood carving saved from some odds and ends. The jade screen now slides up and down within the stand.

164. To decorate the jade screen, we assembled broken pieces of nephrite carvings and fixed them to it with green art gum.

165. Here is our attractive jade table screen, 7 inches tall. Decorations like those used on it can be glued permanently into position with epoxy, but we prefer to change them now and then. In Color Plate 20 the same screen appears with three coral fish as decoration.

If you find that you take to jade carving, you will want to acquire more sophisticated tools such as diamond saws and drills, which will make your work much easier. You may find, too, that you want to join a rock club. At the least, however, even if you never carve more than one piece, you will have learned more about jade, its hardness and toughness, than you could ever learn from mere reading and handling.

166. When we came upon an almost cube-shaped piece of rose quartz, we tried making another peach. The finished fruit has fluorite leaves; it is shown in Color Plate 20.

Another added bonus: Once you have tried working with jade, you will not be afraid to smooth out and polish the chipped corner or edge on your favorite jade or other "pet stone." After all, it is not pleasant to fondle a jade with a sharp edge, and almost all antique or old jades have been dropped frequently enough to have developed such imperfections. If you have worn your jade ring constantly for a number of years and it has begun to look dull and lackluster, it can be polished. First, cover the metal part of the ring with masking tape, leaving only the stone exposed. Then wet some tin oxide and spread it on a piece of clean leather, and polish the stone gently for an hour or so. This will make it as shiny and beautiful as it originally was. But one word of caution: If you are fortunate enough to have an archaic jade, please, please, do *not* do anything to it!

10

Pseudo and Imitation Jades

Pseudojade in this context means "false jade." There are many stones that could be listed under this heading, but *only* those stones that are *frequently and persistently sold, knowingly or unknowingly,* as jade need be discussed here. We have named them in order of their prevalence.

Serpentine (Soochow Jade)

Baffling to most collectors is this stone so much like jade in appearance that even the experts often have to look more than once before deciding whether they have jade or serpentine in their hands. Serpentine is one of the most common of all massive rock formations on earth. Its structural similarity to nephrite has made it one of the favorite stones for decorative purposes in architecture. Great slabs are cut to form indoor entranceways and walls in public buildings. It is referred to as "antique verde" by interior decorators.

The similarity of serpentine to nephrite is not surprising, since the veins of nephrite are almost always sandwiched between masses of it. The color varies from white and a very light celadon green to brown to a black green. The hardness of serpentine can range from 2.5 to 5.

Detecting whether one has a piece of nephrite or serpentine is best done by the scratch test (see Chapter 7).

Bowenite (Soochow Jade, Korean Jade)

A relatively scarce form of serpentine known as bowenite is a waterish yellow green or a beautiful white stone (other colors are less plentiful). It has the same kind of luster as nephrite and is more translucent. White bowenite is so like mutton-fat nephrite jade that it is difficult to tell the difference, but when bowenite is scratched, a white line is left. When you are attracted by an elaborate new carving from the People's Republic of China and you ask the dealer about it, he may tell you that it is "new jade." If it is in the form of an archaic vessel with a long chain of interlocking links, and priced at two hundred to five hundred dollars, you can be sure you are looking at a piece of bowenite or serpentine. A nephrite vessel of that size and workmanship would run into the thousands of dollars.

Aventurine (Indian Jade)

A stone known as aventurine is often spoken of as Indian jade. It is a form of quartz with mica or hematite inclusions that sparkle in the light. The best quality of this quartz has such minute specks in it that one can hardly see them without the use of a magnifier. However, it has a glassy look. The colors range from a light green to a dark bottle green to reddish brown—the natural form of goldstone. It is not very expensive (except the goldstone type, which is rather rare), and a necklace of a hundred beads should not cost much over fifteen or twenty dollars.

Chrysoprase (Australian Jade)

This stone is often mistaken for jadeite. When first introduced into China, it was rejected because it was like no jade the Chinese knew. Chrysoprase is found in many places, but Australia seems to have the most beautiful type. It is a very uniform, pretty green; perhaps bright apple green would describe it. It has a very high luster. In its own right it is a jewel-quality stone, though not jade and not endowed with the qualities of jade. It is a chalcedony formation in the same category as agate, and like agate has a hardness of 6 to 6.5.

Carnelian (Red Jade)

Red agate or carnelian is the stone that is sometimes deliberately used to deceive by calling it red jade. It can readily be detected for what it is—held to the light, it is very uniform; it has no fibrousness, no crystalline quality. It is translucent and pretty, but *not* red jade.

Jasper (Jasper Jade)

This is a form of agate that is called jasper jade when it is green. Most specimens are a very dark green. When it is closely examined, usually red spots can be seen throughout; hence it is more commonly known as bloodstone.

Rhodonite (Pink Jade, Peking Red Jade)

Arriving on the market just recently are small figurines and snuff bottles sometimes labeled as "pink jade." These are rhodonite, a very attractive stone, but not jade; it cannot stand the tests for jade. Usually the stone is a mottled pink and gray.

Thulite (Pink Jade)

Thulite is a pink stone with dark green inclusions that look very like dark green nephrite. It too is sometimes referred to as "pink jade." It is a good stone and worth having in ring or bracelet form. Sometimes a small amount of actual jade is present as inclusions.

Nan-yang yü (Nan-yang Jade or Honan Jade)

There have long been reports of jade "in situ" in China's Honan Province. Professor Arno Schuller of the University of Uppsala made an analysis of this stone and found that it has less than 10 percent jadeite in it. In fact, he has stated that the stone is neither jadeite nor nephrite.* Lapidaries in China today still work this stone called "Nan-yang yü." The material is predominately white or green, or a very interesting patterned white with almost rectangular green spots in it. The stone is more nearly related to diopside than to any other we are familiar with in this country. But there seems not to be a great abundance of it because it is not being exported now and never has been, in any quantity.

Dyed Stones

We must mention briefly a few stones that are dyed to look like jade. Usually, when they are put out for sale, the merchants do not make any pretense that they are jade. These stones are alabaster, marble, and onyx. In the early 1960s Italy exported a great quantity of large oriental-style figurines carved from alabaster, but dyed to simulate jade. In the stores these were clearly marked "alabaster jade," but now they are showing up in antiques shops and flea markets, often with no labels. They have a very uniform color except for a deep green at the inner core, and shade gradually into a translucent green on the outside. The material is very soft and easily scratched. Low-grade onyx from Mexico is sometimes referred to as Mexican jade. It is a soft material that will scratch with a sharp fingernail; it too can be dyed.

---

*S. Howard Hansford, *Chinese Carved Jades* (Greenwich, Conn.: New York Graphic Society, Ltd., 1968), p. 33.

How is the beginner to learn to distinguish these dyed materials from the true jade? He should go to several gem and rock stores, attend a few gem and rock shows, buy a few small items (beads, for instance) and small chunks of raw material. Take them home, study them, try scratching them with a knife. Try sanding them, as described in Chapter 9, "How to Carve Your Own Jade." A little experience of this kind will keep the beginner from making the serious mistake of paying twenty-five to fifty dollars for a bracelet cut from marble and dyed to look like beautiful jade.

Imitation Jades

The buyer of jade, of jewelry, especially, must constantly be aware of imitation jades.

Glass as a substitute for jade came very early in China. Specimens of glass molded into jade ritualistic objects date as far back as the Chou dynasty. Glass beads, bracelets, rings, and other costume jewelry were made to imitate jade, but can be readily recognized for what they are.* Old Chinese glass will show air bubbles and even small specks of clay. Mainland China is now exporting glass objects, and small bubbles are visible in them, but the specks of clay are gone.

Plastics need only be colored a shade of emerald green to entice the buyer. They may give the wearer the fun of fooling most people, but they will not fool the initiated.

Porcelain was often compared to jade; it is even recorded in Chinese chronicles that sometime during the T'ang dynasty porcelain was sent to the emperor as "false jade." Just imagine a bowl made from white clay and covered with a white or celadon glaze that would come from the kiln looking like a magnificent nephrite jade! Such a development was especially important to the Chinese, who had to pay dearly for nephrite. It is perhaps an irony of history that a porcelain bottle of the early Ming period was sold for over a million dollars only a few years ago, but the best-carved and finest-quality jade vase has a long way to go to catch up with such a price. Today it is doubtful that anyone would confuse porcelain with jade.

---

*For further information on this subject, see *Oriental Antiques and Collectibles–A Guide,* by Arthur and Grace Chu (New York: Crown Publishers, Inc., 1973).

11

An Investigation into Dyed Jade

Can jade be dyed? Yes!

Even the diamond can be tinted. The ruby can be heated so that the beautiful color becomes more uniform. Nearly all stones can be treated in one way or another to improve their looks and beauty. Since jade is relatively unstable, it can be dyed to make it take on the look of a priceless gem.

We have already noted that nephrite will become altered or calcified by burial. If it has been through a fire, it will acquire a chicken-bone look, with small shiny blisters on the surface. Jadeite, under high temperature, fuses into a colorless liquid not unlike molten glass.

When a jade boulder falls into a stream and remains there for hundreds of years, it acquires a crust as a result of the action of the chemicals in the water. After being polished or carved, the crust or skin shows beautiful colors. This is a natural process.

What concerns us here is not the natural process, but the process used intentionally by man to enhance the color of the stone or to add color to it, so that it will look more beautiful and can be sold for a higher price. Since this dyeing process takes only hours or days, it is also important to know how long the color can last, and we decided to make an investigation.

The most difficult part of our investigation was to acquire samples. Naturally there is no jewelry store in the whole world that advertises dyed jade. When you walk into a store specializing in jade and ask the proprietor if he has any dyed jade, the answer is always, "I don't know what you mean." Then he is ready to show you the door. To a jade merchant, "dyed" is a dirty word. It could entirely ruin his business.

After many failures, we were about to give up the investigation when, through a pawnbroker, we met a man who had dyed jade to sell at his home.

"I really do not own these jades," he kept telling us as he opened a box containing thousands of beautiful newly cut cabochons of three different sizes. The color of the stones ranged from apple green to deep resonant forest green. They were very attractive.

"I don't know anything about jade," he continued. "You see, a sailor borrowed some money from me, and left these as surety. But he never returned, so I have to sell them to get my money back."

"How much do you want for each one?"

"Ten dollars apiece." He paused. "But if you buy a large quantity, I can give you a very reasonable wholesale price."

"How many do we have to buy?"

"At least a hundred."

"How about fifty?"

"That—" He hesitated. "All right. But there can be no refund once the stones are out of my door. As I said already, I know nothing about jade. I only want to get my money back."

We brought the cabochons home and examined them more closely. They were all a beautiful green and of gem quality. Two or three pieces had a slightly unnatural blue green color.

First, we put half of them into a pan of water and slowly brought the water to a boil. After an hour, we took the stones out. The water was green, but when we compared these stones with the unboiled ones, there was no visible difference in their appearance. We boiled them again and again, for three hours and then for nearly a whole day. The water continued to show a slight green color, but there was never a noticeable loss of color in the stones. Next, we soaked them overnight in full-strength laundry bleach. Again, there was no change of color. Finally, we tried 20-percent-volume peroxide, and the result was the same.

Suspecting that the stones were dyed only superficially, we had one cut. To our surprise, it was dyed to the core.

We taped a couple of pieces onto a windowpane where they would receive sunlight almost the whole day. After eight months of the hot late spring, summer, and fall sunshine, the color had turned very dark and the stones had lost their prettiness.

Now there remained just one last experiment: We put a few stones into boiling oil, at approximately the temperature used for making French fried potatoes. After five minutes, the color began to lighten, but the stones were still green. After ten minutes, however, they had become well-polished, well-cut, pristine-white cabochons of jadeite.

We could not find any lavender jade to use for experiment, but according to a friend who did, the color looks rather unnatural but lasts longer than the green—almost indefinitely.

So here are our conclusions, based on our investigation:

If you pay one hundred dollars or more for a uniformly green jade ring or pendant, and the jade is a dyed one, even if it is set in 14k gold, you are being robbed. When you buy, you should get at least a 24-hour money-back guarantee—particularly if your stone is a newly cut one. Old rings with old stones are almost never dyed. Nor is a stone that has two or more colors—for instance, one that is partly green and partly white. Dyed jades are always one solid color.

As soon as you get home, test your stone. Don't boil it in either oil or water—jade is heat-sensitive and, at least theoretically, boiling can hurt it. Just put your ring or stone in a white porcelain cup of clear hot water—the water to be no hotter than a cup of coffee you can drink. Use as small a cup as possible, just large enough to contain the ring or stone and keep it submerged. Leave it for twelve hours or overnight. If the stone is dyed, you will detect a tinge of green in the water after the time has elapsed.

If you have paid only ten or fifteen dollars for an attractive jade that has been set, say, in a 10k gold-filled ring, don't worry about it even if it proves to be a dyed stone. As long as you don't accidentally drop it into the oil while you are making French fried potatoes—and don't sunbathe it for months from sunrise to sunset—the stone will maintain its color for five, ten, or maybe twenty years. And that's good enough for an investment of ten or fifteen dollars. Even costume jewelry costs more. One reminder, though: Any expensive piece of jade, particularly a ring or a bracelet, that constantly touches other objects, should not be worn all the time—not, for instance, while dishwashing, cooking, or driving. It will slowly but surely get a worn look and lose its beauty. Even a diamond can get dull with continuous wear.

Finally, there is the often-asked but quite pertinent question: What percentage of jewel jades are dyed?

No one really knows. Some put it at 50 percent, others, at less than one tenth of one percent. We think both figures can be right. If you buy at a reputable store whose stock in trade consists mainly of jade, and you have a money-back guarantee even for a day or two—enough time for you to make a simple test—you have no worry. But it pays to make the test anyway. We know of one woman who bought a bracelet from a large store that is noted for its integrity. Later on, the woman showed it to an expert, and one thing led to another; the bracelet was proved to be dyed. The woman took it back to the store, and the salesman sent the bracelet upstairs to their experts. A few minutes later, the manager himself came down and invited her into his office. "I'm afraid our buyer has goofed," he confessed. Then, with profuse apologies, he gave her a refund and personally saw her to the door. "I was treated like a VIP," said the erstwhile irate but now satisfied customer.

On the other hand, if someone appears out of nowhere and offers to sell you a jade ring for fifty dollars that is purported to be worth five hundred dollars—because he is suddenly faced with a need for money, or for some other lame reason—you have a fifty-fifty chance of buying a dyed stone that is worth less than five dollars.

During World War II, many American soldiers in Burma spent a great deal of their pay buying the famous Burmese rubies to bring home as gifts for their wives, girl friends, or mothers. The stones were big and beautiful, and the price was more than reasonable. After they got back home and took their rubies to their jewelers to be set into rings or bracelets, they were shocked to be told that their gems were mere glass. This at least solved one of the mysteries of the Burma campaign: the frequent disappearance of rear jeep lights!

12
Jade Throughout the World

After having been introduced to the jade of the Forbidden City, the reader may be reluctant to go on a prosaic tour of the world's sources of jade. Actually, jade is not uncommon. There is an abundance of it—that is, an abundance of nephrite. Jadeite of the kind found in Burma has been located in only a few places outside that country, and only Burma can claim a plentiful supply of high-quality jadeite. With this in mind, we will start first in a place close to China.

Russia

In Russia, around the west end of Lake Baikal in Siberia, a large quantity of nephrite is quarried. The color ranges from a yellow green to a deep green. It is very translucent, but it does have inclusions of chromite in small specks. (These inclusions used to be considered graphite, but are now identified as chromite.) However, it is possible to extract cabochons of good size that have only microscopic inclusions. This jade makes good decorative pieces, and the Chinese used it during the Ch'ing dynasty for large carvings. They particularly enjoyed the specimens that were produced in a material with dark splotches, like small water plants floating in sea green water. Carl Fabergé, the famous designer of the crown jewels for the last czar and czarina of Russia, created many pieces from Siberian nephrite in his workshop in Saint Petersburg.

Japan

For many years there was controversy surrounding the claims of nephrite or jadeite having been found in Japan. This controversy occurred because, at ancient gravesites in Japan, a few pieces of jadeite carved into small comma-shaped and cylindrical beads were found, and assumptions were immediately made that jadeite was available to the Japanese from their own islands. Even Japanese scholars believed, however, that the pieces in question must have come from China because Japan had traded with China for many centuries. Nevertheless, in 1953, jadeite was discovered "in situ" in Japan. The locality was in Niigata Prefecture, where a small industry of hard-stone carving existed. None of this material was ever exported, since it was a very small vein to begin with.

167. A ram made of Taiwan jade, medium to dark green in color, with black inclusions.

Taiwan

Sometime after the mainland Chinese settled on the island of Taiwan and set up the Republic of China, a large deposit of nephrite was discovered on the eastern side of the island. Upon examination, much of the material seemed too soft to be jade. However, chemical analysis showed it to be nephrite. Currently, Taiwan lapidaries are carving not only the best of their own stone but a good deal from British Columbia.

New Zealand

New Zealand produces a nephrite of quite uniform color. It is a good leaf green; perhaps "camellia green" would best describe its color. It is quite translucent and relatively free from inclusions. The most famous objects made from New Zealand nephrite are the "hei tiki" gods of the

Maoris. They are a unique human form with the head tilted to one side. These little pieces have a happy, carefree quality that fascinates most people, especially archeologists. Although it is true that these jade gods are worn as amulets to fend off evil, and the Maoris do think of jade as having medicinal powers, they do not—in contrast with the Chinese —have that really serious belief in it as a stone surpassing all others in worth. There is ample evidence that the early Stone Age Maori people used the pebbles that were washed up on the beaches or that tumbled down the mountainsides into the riverbeds. Archeological evidence points to the possibility that the Maoris brought nephrite artifacts with them from New Caledonia during their migration. Some of these same artifacts have been uncovered in New Guinea, and nephrite "in situ" is on both islands. Simple tools made of jade can be found and purchased from the Maoris even now. It is almost certain that these early tools were also used for the simple carving of jade.

British Columbia

From the Fraser River bed in Canada the Indians of North America have always been able to get nephrite. Large tools were shaped from it. Unfortunately, the jade is usually of a very dark green and often specked with graphite inclusions, although when the best color is found, it can be very desirable. Large quantities are now being shipped to Taiwan and Hong Kong. It is known that Canada has massive boulders of this nephrite, but it is difficult to get out of the far recesses of the country.

United States

Eskimos have long used the Alaskan nephrite for making tools, especially small pieces that could be sharpened and fastened to bone or wood to be used as spearheads and knives. There is little evidence that the Eskimos attached any supernatural qualities to jade, but they did have an almost worshipful attitude toward the Jade Mountain from which it came. And they appreciated the jade color, a Kelly green, quite uniform. An American explorer, Lieutenant George M. Stoney of the United States Navy (1835–86), found the Jade Mountain in the remote areas of northern Alaska by following the Kobuk River to its source. At the time, great boulders were hauled away, but because jade has never held the mystique for North Americans that it has for the Chinese, a constant supply is not always needed. However, the amateur jade hunter finds the hazardous trip to the source of Alaskan jade well worth the effort.

There are several other states in the United States where jade has been found. However, there are only two places where the amount available has been of equal interest to the lapidary; one of them, Wyoming, has a highly prized black jade, a nephrite. Polished to a high gloss, a pure black Wyoming jade is incomparable. This is a fine jewel jade and worth a good price. However, much of it does have inclusions of iron pyrites. These look like bright streaks of silver against the mirror-black background. This nephrite not only is tough, but has a hardness at the upper end of the scale for nephrite. Several other colors are also found in Wyoming, including an apple green, but they are not plentiful.

168. Botryoidal jade, popularly known as grape jade, from California. After digging out the serpentine from these pieces, we tried to imagine the different things they might become. The jade on the left was made into a grape cluster; it appears in Color Plate 19. The piece in the center looks like a Buddha's-hand citron, and the one at right like a sitting old man.

169. California jadeite. This jadeite has too many inclusions and it undercuts badly. Shown here are a slab of this jade and a knife carved by the authors.

California is the other state noted for its many deposits of nephrite. One widely known to the general public is at Jade Cove in the Los Padres National Park, on the Pacific coast south of scenic Monterey. This jade, like the green jade of British Columbia or Wyoming, is a dark green. "Rock hounds" enjoy exploring the shore for it, and skin divers have brought up sizeable boulders off the coast.

California has two or three places where jadeite can be found. One of these is at Clear Creek, a town on the Eel River north of San Francisco. The quality is hardly of jewel standard, but small cabochons can be cut from it. It is an interesting jadeite in that it is layered in uneven streaks with serpentine and other minerals. The jadeite is difficult to separate from other deposits, but large thin slabs have been used for lamp shades or even for small windows where the light can filter through all the variations of green and reveal the formation of the stone. At this same location specimens of chloromelanite, a variety of jadeite, were discovered. Chloromelanite is always a very dark green black.

In California can be found still another form of jade, botryoidal nephrite. (See Ill. 168.)

The places named are those where jade is plentiful enough to make it worthwhile for amateurs to go prospecting for it. However, there have been confirmed reports of finds also in Washington, Michigan, New York, Wisconsin, Utah, and Oregon.

Central and South America

In 1955 the source of the jadeite used by the Mayas was discovered in Guatemala, and today a large boulder from there resides in the Smithsonian Institution in Washington, D.C. Examination of the stone proved it to be chloromelanite. Guatemalan jadeite has not yet come to the marketplace.

We can only speculate about the artifacts remaining from the lost Mayan civilization. Very few pieces have been found in good condition, although the marvelous mask shown in *Smithsonian* magazine of April 1977 attests to the fact that the Mayas had certainly learned to use their jadeite well. The quality of the stone is not comparable to that found in Burma, as it has many inclusions; it is said to have crystals as large as a half inch in size meshed with others in an interlocking formation.

Though the word "jade" is almost synonymous with "China," it is from explorations in this part of the Western world that the word eventually came into the English language. When Cortes returned with treasure from the New World sometime between 1528 and 1530, he had with him pieces of the green stone for the people in Spain to see. At that time the stone was given its Western name, "piedra de ijada." The English word "jade" is reported to have come from a misprinting of the French translation. Because the explorers had gone to the New World seeking gold, interest in the beautiful green stone that they brought home was minimal until they told their countrymen how the New World natives used it as medicine.

Central America, then, becomes the third best known place in the world where jade was found and used. In Brazil and Argentina and in the West Indies, new explorations have uncovered both jadeite and nephrite.

Europe

Stone Age man found jadeite here and made it into tools. Some of these have been uncovered in the Swiss lake region. It is thought that boulders were washed down from the mountains. There were reports of jadeite being sent from the Bavarian region to China years ago, to be carved, but the Chinese did not find it a pleasing stone and rejected further shipments of it. However, deposits of jade of the nephrite variety have been discovered in several localities in Europe.

Africa

Southern Rhodesia has just recently become a source of jadeite. Reports of its quality are not immediately available.

The British Isles

It is known that Scotland, England, and Ireland produce nephrite. Theirs, however, is not jade of commercial value, although celts of good-quality nephrite have been uncovered in diggings in the British Isles.

Burma

Just to make the world survey complete, we must say again that Burma is the only present source of fine-quality jadeite.

13
The Jade Smuggling General

During World War II, when lend-lease was approved for China, the Japanese had already occupied the entire coast. The only seaport available was Rangoon in Burma, and the trickle of military supplies, properly termed too little and too late, had to go by convoys of trucks up the tortuous Burma Road. When Japan attacked Pearl Harbor, her military forces made a sweeping move to swallow all southeast Asia, an area rich in rice and other resources. But her major objective was to close the Burma Road, thereby forcing China to her knees. Japan then could transfer most of her military forces out of the stalemated area and use them against the Allies.

If the Burma Road was lost, China's last lifeline would be gone. This was indeed a threat of unprecedented proportions, and China had to guard against it. Burma was under British control. So the Chinese proposed a joint defense. But the British, so occupied elsewhere that they could not see a way to defend Burma, indulged in foot-dragging. Finally, the Chinese told the British in no uncertain terms that they would send their own armies in. Afraid of losing her postwar claim to the territory, Britain reluctantly agreed to supply provisions, a small number of armed forces, and an administrative staff, to help the joint campaign.

This was the agreement, but it worked out very badly. The British administrative staff left before the arrival of Chinese forces, thus depriving the latter of supplies and intelligence; and the small contingent of British forces steered clear of contact with the enemy, to avoid losses.

When the battle was joined, the Japanese had all the advantages. The Chinese army was cut in two—one part retreated back into Yunnan, China, and the other into India. China lost her last supply line.

Should China try to reopen the Burma Road?

General Stillwell said, "Yes." But the Chinese government, supported by General Chennault, opposed the idea. Their argument was that since the quantity of lend-lease allotted to China was very small, it could be flown in "over the hump," and be used immediately to fight the Japanese. So why fly Chinese soldiers into India to join the remnants there, spend the lend-lease allotment to equip them, and then waste months training them to retake the Burma Road? But since Stillwell was the ranking general and represented the United States, he had the say. After months of training and months of hard fighting, the Burma Road was retaken. It was renamed Stillwell Road, although the general had been transferred by that time, for diplomatic reasons.

This historical summary makes it clear that Burma, the place that produces the world's most beautiful jade, was for several years ravaged by war. The quarrying of raw jade was entirely stopped, and the supply was at an all-time low when the war ended in 1945. Burma achieved her independence after the war. Realizing that her neighbor, China, had never produced enough of her famed nephrite for export, and that there would be a great demand for the scarce jadeite, the Burmese government contemplated nationalization of jade quarrying and making jade a government monopoly. However, she was prevented from carrying out her plan because of the arrival of uninvited "guests."

Burma could not oust her uninvited guests because they were quite numerous and equipped with modern weapons. They were the armies of the Nationalist government, driven out of China by the Communist forces. Having no other place to go, the remnants of the once-large land army had crossed the border into Burma and set up housekeeping in the mountainous region where the best of the world's jadeite was and is produced. And since these soldiers were no longer paid by their government on Taiwan, they had to do something to make a living. It happened that the region they occupied was most suitable for opium culture, so they started planting poppies and harvesting the raw opium. For years they smuggled it out into southwest Asia, and lived very well from the profits.

Then came the Vietnam war. Many American soldiers were enticed into trying the drug, and they became addicted. The worried American military authorities found out where the opium came from, and decided that the only remedy was to root out the source. They used the standard American method, which sometimes works and sometimes doesn't—that is, to subsidize the planters and extract their promise to give up planting the crop, as has been done in Turkey and elsewhere.

Several military intelligence officers were dispatched to northern Burma. They met the commander—we'll call him General Li—whose troops were busily engaged in cutting open the poppy seed pods and collecting the juice. The Americans were cordially invited into the general's house and treated as guests of honor. They explained the purpose of their visit and presented their proposal: If General Li's troops would stop planting opium, the United States government would pay him many millions of dollars.

The general at once accepted their proposal, and next day arranged a ceremony as solemn as the signing of a diplomatic treaty. In the presence of the American visitors, a contingent of his soldiers marched in carrying covered bamboo baskets on poles. They emptied the contents of the baskets onto a pile of kindling wood. The general proposed a toast to the well-being of his honorable American guests and then touched a lighted match to the pile. As smoke and flames shot up, the air became filled with a not unpleasant odor that gave the Americans a strange feeling, almost a sense of euphoria.

The general raised his glass. "This smoke and flame, gentlemen, represents our entire last crop. Had you gentlemen not come, it would have been in Vietnam in about six weeks."

At this point, one of the Americans decided that the general ought to be asked for some sort of guarantee.

"General Li," he began, "how are you and your men going to make a living if you stop planting opium?"

"I'll tell you a secret, my friend." The general lowered his voice. "As you know, our occupation is smuggling—and we will continue to smuggle."

"But we are paying you—"

"Excuse me a moment, my friend." The general went out, then returned with two pieces of rock, one green and one lavender.

"It's jade, the Stone of Heaven," he said as he rubbed the stones lovingly. "All around here, in the mountains and in the streams, you can find it everywhere. I have heard that the price for raw jade is very high. When we begin to smuggle out jade, there will be a big market—we'll get even more money. I will say, though, it is much harder work than planting opium. These rocks are hard to break and heavy to transport, but my men need exercise. They are getting lazy planting opium, and some of them are getting the bad habit of smoking the stuff."

The general stood up. Then he spoke again. "Ah, yes, with Western friends—although my word alone is good as gold—I have learned that you like to have a guarantee."

"That is our custom," one of the Americans agreed.

"Well, I propose that you take my number one son with you. If I break my word—"

"You mean as hostage?"

"Precisely. If I break my word, you can starve him, you can torture him—"

"No, no! In our country, we do not—"

"Now, please do me this favor. You see, my son is over twenty, and in this country he cannot get an education. So I am asking you to do me the favor of taking him as both hostage and student, so that he can study in

America. I hope he can become an engineer and make a good living. There is no future for him in Burma. My friend, I am trying to kill two birds with one stone."

"In that case, we will certainly see what we can do. But not as a hostage. This must be understood."

Raw jadeite became more and more plentiful—the general was certainly doing a good job of smuggling it out. However, the quantity of opium coming from the area never seemed to decrease. Did the general break his word?

An overseas newspaper correspondent got in touch with him.

"I swear to heaven I have never broken my word," the general declared. But he seemed bitter and downcast. "Look all over my area and see if you can find one opium poppy. But two or three miles from here there is another army under the command of another general. I have no control over him or them. I thought the Americans had also spoken to them, but apparently not. So they are still planting and smuggling. I don't want to try to stop them and start a civil war—I've been through too many civil wars already. And of course the natives are still planting opium. As far as I am concerned, my word is always as good as solid gold. I am proud to tell anybody that I am now the smuggler of the Stone of Heaven!"

14
Other Materials Used for Carvings

Limestone and Sandstone

Only in museums can we see the massive sculptured Buddhas that were hacked from the cliff sides, or the tediously carved steles stolen from the caves of faraway places of China. But for those who have doubted the ability of the Chinese to execute the human physique in stone or clay, one need only view a lone hand of a Buddha in sandstone to recognize the artistic and realistic quality of the work of the early sculptors.

Marble

Marble is not generally thought of as one of the stones the Chinese used for ornamental carving, but it was chiseled and sculptured as early as the Shang and pre-Shang periods. Most people would be familiar with it as insets for screens, couches, chairs, and tables. The pieces were chosen for their markings, which look like Chinese brush landscape paintings. These are called "Ta-Li" marble, and are from Yunnan Province. We have seen small sets of cups and saucers tooled from marble that have the feel of unglazed porcelain. They were carved very thin, and consequently are quite translucent and are easily mistaken for Chinese glass. Today, the Chinese are working and exporting marble. Their large white Dogs of Fo are attractive; the marble bracelets and beads have been dyed and treated to look very much like jadeite.

170. An intricate carving done on a black slatelike stone called river stone in the United States. It is often used to make ink-stones. *Dr. and Mrs. Marvin Hockabout*

Soapstone

The popularity of soapstone (talc) carvings here in America is incomprehensible to the Chinese, who have always considered them as something to buy from a vendor when on a holiday, and to be discarded before the next holiday rolls around and new soapstone pieces are purchased. To the westerner, however, soapstone has considerable appeal. Often it is skillfully carved. One of the favorite carvings (and soapstone can be literally "carved" with a sharp tool) is of monkeys climbing and playing around a vase. Good-quality soapstone (if it can be said that there is such a thing) was often used for making seals for the Chinese. The very difficulty of carving a seal requires a material that is not too hard. It must be carved in high relief, and the letters or characters have to be reversed, just as they are on our rubber stamps. Seals of soapstone would last almost a lifetime because, after use, they were always placed carefully in a box. If one was dropped and broken in two, a little glue of almost any type would restore it.

Collectors of Chinese seals should beware of being conned into thinking they are buying a jade seal.

Steatite is a soapstone, and the term is heard occasionally. Soochow jade can refer to soapstone or serpentine.*

---

*Soochow jade, as was mentioned in *Oriental Antiques and Collectibles — a Guide*, by the authors, is also used as a derogatory reference to an individual who is considered weak either morally or physically.

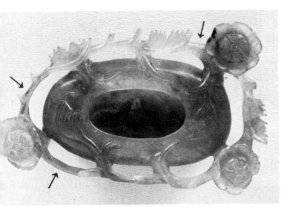 

171. A bowenite water coup. Parts of the rim (indicated by arrows) had been broken and were restored with epoxy by the authors.

172. A bowlful of delectable fruit. The grape clusters, from light to dark, are bowenite, carnelian, and aventurine. Other fruits and leaves are made from pieces of serpentine of various colors. *Colonel and Mrs. George Fong*

Serpentine

This stone has been discussed in the chapter on pseudojades. However, it might be well here to say that serpentine has long been worked into quite elaborate and decorative pieces by the Chinese. When highly polished, it has good luster. Various shades of white and light celadon are carved for insets in boxes and for wall plaques. A frequent use of serpentine during the age of the greatest export trade from China to the United States (from about 1918 to 1938) was for small or medium-sized table screens and mirror backs. These pieces were cut rather thin and then encrusted with coral, malachite, lapis, dark green serpentine, and glass, to form pictures. (Much soapstone was utilized this way too.) The serpentine plaques were made from two inches to about ten inches in diameter. A few merchants will insist that these are jade, but very little jade actually was used in this way. Many so-called jade trees may have flowers made of combinations of semiprecious stone, with serpentine leaves. Fruits, such as some of those in Ill. 172, are very often sculptured from serpentine.

Bowenite

Bowenite is a term used only since the nineteenth century, after G. T. Bowen recognized a compact form of serpentine that is uniform in color, either white or light green, and has a hardness up to 6 on the Mohs scale. A translucent white bowenite made into beads and small decorative pieces is coming from Korea today, and dealers sometimes unknowingly refer to these as made of Korean jade. Large carvings of bowenite now coming from mainland China are of a light, almost chartreuse, green. It is a beautiful stone in its own right, and the Chinese find it very satisfying for their creative productions.

173. A covered jar with handles and free rings, carved very thin in the Mogul style. It is made of a clam-broth-colored agate, very much like translucent nephrite. *Dr. and Mrs. Marvin Hockabout*

174. Carnelian figurine. *Dr. and Mrs. Marvin Hockabout*

175. A ram and a dog, both of carnelian.

Agate

Carnelian agate is probably one of the favorite stones of the Chinese for working into ornamental pieces. Today there is a good deal of this stone on the market, and much of it is so uniform in color that one recognizes it has been treated. If the stone in its natural form has red in it, together with white or gray, it need only be heated to a high temperature for the red to disperse evenly throughout the stone.

Other colors of agate are often seen. The clam-broth type (Ill. 173) is beautiful in small free-ringed cups and can easily be mistaken for jade in the Indian type of carving, as described in Chapter 15. Still other colors are carved into snuff bottles, where the variations in each piece are cleverly utilized to make the design stand out. Note also the figure shown in Ill. 174.

Quartz

Almost every museum has one carving of pure, clear quartz crystal. The huge water buffalo at the Center for Asian Art and Culture at the de Young Museum in San Francisco is a good example. It is possible to find on the market small items carved of quartz—Kwan-yins, fish, vases. Since all colors of quartz are used, it is not necessary to list each under a separate category—that is, amethyst, rose, smoky, green, and blue quartz. Quartz with rutile inclusions or hair crystal was often used for snuff bottles.

Fluorite

The Chinese recognized the beauty of this stone and made it into interesting pieces. The ones most commonly seen are in a blue green, but some blend from magenta to green to lavender and brown. Fluorite was carved into both vessels and figurines, and Americans have often made these into lamp bases. Its disadvantages are the cleavages that not only interfere with carving, but frequently make a piece appear cracked and ready to fall apart. Breakage is also a constant problem for the lapidary. Many of the surviving pieces that are seen on the market today have suffered damage and been repaired. Their value is questionable, but the beauty of the cube-shaped crystals and the transparent coloring never fails to appeal.

176. A vase of rock crystal, 5½ inches high. *Dr. and Mrs. Marvin Hockabout*

177. Rose of green aventurine on a blackwood stand.

Above left:
178. Amethyst figurine. *Dr. and Mrs. Marvin Hockabout*

Above right:
179. Poinsettia plants of rose quartz with leaves and pots of spinach green jade. *Colonel and Mrs. George Fong*

Right:
180. A rose quartz covered vase in floral design with a green fluorite stand. *Dr. and Mrs. Marvin Hockabout*

Turquoise

In China, the earliest use of turquoise was as inlays in the archaic bronze vessels or in the bronze handles of the ritualistic jade weapons. Turquoise is found in almost every country. It has been made into decorative items by prehistoric people all over the world. Relatively soft (4 to 6 on the Mohs scale), it is easy to work. The Chinese prized the type with the thin black lines they called spider web, which comes mostly from the Tibetan region. Much of the robin's-egg blue variety was sent to China from Iran. Mainland China has recently exported necklaces of this particular color of turquoise. Whether it is of native origin or imported from other countries is not known. Turquoise figurines and old snuff bottles are highly regarded and quite expensive. Many pieces of inexpensive jewelry for export, however, were encrusted with turquoise. Substituting glass for turquoise was also practiced. Much of the turquoise on the market in the United States now is said to be "reinforced." This means that a resin compound in liquid form has been applied to the stone so that it can seep down into the crevices and tiny cracks and strengthen the turquoise. However, high-quality turquoise does not need to be treated.

Malachite

This beautiful green stone, relatively soft (3 to 4 on the Mohs scale), is another favorite of the Chinese. It was worked into "mountains," vases, and small decorative pieces, as well as inexpensive jewelry. Snuff bottles and figurines were also made. People occasionally confuse malachite with turquoise, but the striated markings on the malachite are easily seen, and distinguish it from a deep green turquoise.

181A. A smoky quartz figure of Bodhidharma, the founder of Ch'an Buddhism, on an amethyst base.

181B. Fluorite vase with hydra decoration.

182. *a.* Turquoise male child, 2 inches, with a carp, which symbolizes a high position and a distinguished career for the boy. The child's figure can be considered a fertility symbol. *b.* Reverse of the same figure. Note that the body shape is that of a baby; the head, large in proportion to the body, as a baby's head is, is shaped more like that of an adult. The face has the expression of an adult and baby combined.

183. Snuff bottle made by the authors. The authors made this bottle with epoxy putty colored to resemble the gray white matrix. Roughly shaped leaves, tendrils, and grapes were epoxied to the bottle. After shaping them with an emery board and giving them a final polishing, we had what appears to be a carved turquoise snuff bottle—until you look into the interior.

184. Lapis brush rest, carved by the authors.

Lapis Lazuli

Lapis is an opaque blue stone that has been used since prehistoric times as a semiprecious stone. It has a hardness of 5 to 5.5 on the Mohs scale, and is quite available in all countries. Its one drawback is that it is encased in so much gray white chalky rock. Usually the Chinese carved it into mountains and figures as well as beads and small pieces. It can be found made into cabochons for rings and as insets in other old jewelry.

It should be mentioned here that since lapis is in vogue at the present time, its price seems to be unreasonably high.

Sodalite

Sodalite is mentioned here only because today the Chinese are exporting quite large carvings as well as jewelry of this material. It is somewhat more purple than lapis and has inclusions that show up in white streaks. These inclusions are in no set pattern, but tend to give the piece an overall gray blue appearance.

Glass

Glass carvers must employ all the techniques and tools used by the glyptic workers. However, Chinese glass is softer than most stones. Except for very thick glass, it is quite fragile. This explains why most carved glass comes with thick walls. The simplest work was performed on layered glass. It was faceted into diamond-shaped sections that resulted in a harlequin plaid. Large and small vases and jars were made in this way. Snuff bottles with quite intricate designs were a favorite item for the glass carver. It is possible to have the glass layered and ground away to achieve various designs in cameo. Although figurines are often made in soapstone or serpentine, they were almost never made from glass (except small figures to attach to trinket jewelry), and, when they were, they were made in a mold. Perhaps this is so because, in spite of the arduous care taken to sculpt a figurine, the breakage rate was too great. But bowls, jars, vases, and even candle holders can still be found in carved glass, often imitating jade.

Coral

Strictly speaking, coral is the hornlike substance resulting from the accumulation of skeletons of small marine animals. The Chinese have found that carving the larger pieces into figurines can achieve breathtakingly beautiful results. Red coral is the favorite; the pink, white, and black are less valuable.

Glass is the material most often used to imitate coral, but recently plastic has become a constant hazard for the collector because it imitates the semimatte surface of coral. Therefore, the buyer needs to examine carefully all that is purported to be coral.

Perhaps a word should be said about identifying coral. If the piece is reasonably large, lines similar to the growth lines of a tree trunk or the natural lines on ivory can be seen through a magnifier. Even on a small piece, tiny holes can usually be detected. After you have the item home, the point of a red-hot needle can be pushed against the base or the back of the piece. Coral will scarcely allow a prick, but the needle will sink into plastic and make an unpleasant smell.

Amber

Amber, in all its varieties and its substitutes, is a substance found among Chinese carvings, but natural amber figurines, snuff bottles, and beads carved in China are usually hard to find and very expensive. The best-quality amber is believed to have come to China from the northern coast of

Europe, although Burma supplied a good red variety. It is said that as early as the sixth century China had learned how to make a substitute amber. Therefore, it is necessary to discuss briefly the whole "amber problem," for it is indeed a difficult material for the collector. Below are listed the various tests for amber, starting with the simplest and concluding with those requiring the collector to buy the item and take it home for further testing.

1.   The first, the essential, test is to find out whether the piece develops a negative charge of electricity when rubbed. If small pieces of paper can be picked up by the amber after rubbing it on your sleeve (right while you are talking with the shopkeeper), you will know that it has passed the basic MUST test.

2.   After rubbing the amber, smell it. The odor should be pleasant. Plastic and celluloid have an acrid and very distinctive odor. Amber of all types has a slightly "woodsy" smell. If it has a strong turpentine or pine-pitch smell, it could be new resin rather than amber.

3.   Rub the piece again and immediately put it against the underside of your forearm. As amber is a poor conductor of heat, the warmth retained by amber can be felt.

185.   A Buddha's-hand citron made of greenish yellow amber.

186.   Amber snuff bottle in the shape of a Buddha's-hand citron, carved by the authors.

187.   Amber Buddha's-hand citron snuff bottle of a more rounded shape, carved by the authors.

188.   Amber pendants carved by the authors.

189. Peach carved by the authors from a piece of old Baltic amber of a rich reddish brown.

The preceding three tests should be made right on the spot, when one is thinking of buying amber—whether it is being sold as antique or whether the dealer claims it is recently mined amber. There are bright orange red snuff bottles and figurines on the market today that will fail these tests for the simple reason that they are synthetic. Here is probably the best place to remind the reader that large, clear hunks of amber are very rare and have always been expensive. It simply is not possible for thousands of large amber items to become suddenly available! Also, *complete* insects are rare in true amber, but often appear in abundance in imitation amber.

Amber shavings left after the best of the material is used can be clarified and dyed. This substance is, in essence, amber, but it should be designated as reconstituted or restructured amber, sometimes referred to as "ambroid." In the latter half of the nineteenth century, in France, there was invented a process of heating amber particles by high compression to form large pieces. Much amber of this type was then sent in blocks to China to be carved into small items like snuff bottles or beads.

If you are considering buying beads, make one other observation before making your decision. Look at the drilling around the holes. The beads should not have any type of mold mark or solidified liquid folds at the outer ends of the holes.

In addition to amber from the Baltic Sea area, there is amber from Roumania, Sicily, Burma, Mexico, Korea, and Japan, as well as some from the southern coast of China. Even a few places in the United States have amber. Mining of amber in the Dominican Republic is a relatively new industry. And amber from each source has its own characteristics and color.

Sometimes a claim is made that a particular strand of beads is green amber. Actually, very little green amber was and is mined. Also, now and then someone will swear that he has a strand of black amber beads. The blackness is something that develops after the amber is mined. (Most black amber coming from mines or the sea is brackish and not fit for carving.) Red amber that has been exposed to light a great deal will gradually turn dark on the outer surface. If true amber beads are black on the outside, you need only hold them to the light to see the red color deep inside. Beware, however, of hand-carved beads and figurines from China made from 1900 to about 1938 that are very dark on the outside, but when held to the light show a rich red inside. These are a petroleum product; they were well carved and are definitely a collectible, but they are *not* amber. One should probably refer to them as colophony (rosin). New Buddhist rosaries of colophony have recently shown up on the market. They are hand-tooled, as were the old ones of the same material. These rosaries and figurines will not exhibit static electricity, and when particles are burned the smell is very acrid.

190. Since jade is such expensive material, even the small chips are used, as here, for making things like this flower tree with green serpentine leaves. This tree, set in a frame, was made for export. The stones are crudely cut and polished only slightly.

191. An inkstone carved with a sacred mushroom and a hare, which, according to mythology, lives on the moon under the cassia tree. This tree symbolizes high official position and distinction. The inkstone is very important to scholars and literati, and deserves the most tasteful treatment. The best inkstones were made from the rocks of the Tuan River.

192. An exquisitely carved malachite vase with cover. Height, about 10 inches. *Dr. and Mrs. Marvin Hockabout*

193. Large amethyst floral-carved vase with cover. *Dr. and Mrs. Marvin Hockabout*

Another substance that is mistakenly called amber is horn. One day we saw a carved water buffalo on a shelf in an antique shop. It was labeled "amber." When we examined it, we found it to be dyed yak horn. The price was $235!

If you have a strand of relatively old black beads and it feels too light to be glass—and you are certain it is not plastic—perhaps it is a string of jet beads. Jet is a kind of bituminous coal, very tough, that was made into mourning jewelry during the time of Queen Victoria, after the death of her beloved consort Prince Albert. Black beads became so popular that the Murano glassmakers produced black glass beads that resembled jet, and these too became known as jet beads. This is mentioned here only because some people, even dealers, call jet black amber.

If you decide to take the risk of buying something purported to be amber, after you get it home you can make these additional tests:

4. With a sharp knife (carvers do actually carve amber; it can be sanded, too), try to scrape some tiny particles off the base of the piece or from a hole in a bead. It should not peel, but should come off in small particles. Put these on a piece of foil and burn them. (Use foil because it does not have an odor of its own.) When lighting the match, hold it at arm's length; then bring it slowly to the amber because you do not want your nostrils to pick up the odor of sulphur from the match. When the amber particles burn, a sooty black smoke arises within a second or so. At this time it will exude a pleasant fragrance and make the nostrils tingle a little.

5. Make a mixture of salt and water. Let as much salt dissolve as the water will take before putting the piece of amber into the solution. If it floats (the specific gravity of amber is 1.05 to 1.10), you can be reasonably optimistic. If it sinks with a thud and stays there, it is not amber. Rinse off the salt water and dry the piece immediately. If you are testing a bead, be sure there is no air in the hole to give it buoyancy. Insert a toothpick in the hole; then immerse the bead and remove the toothpick.

And now for the last, a very crucial test:

6. Moisten a tissue with a few drops of rubbing alcohol and dab it on the base of the piece or on one bead up close to the clasp where the test will not show. Baltic amber will not be affected. Other true ambers will be, but not to the extent that anything can be seen or felt. If the area becomes sticky, then the material is no doubt a resin compound. Substitutes that should have been eliminated in the successive tests are not affected by alcohol.

We have scarcely begun to touch the elusive and fascinating subject of amber. Interested readers should avail themselves of Max Bauer's *Precious Stones*, vol. 2, and those issues of the *Bead Journal* with articles by Jamey D. Allen (see Bibliography).

We have tried in this chapter to mention the most commonly known stones carved by the Chinese through the centuries. Obviously we may have missed some that might have been discussed, such as tourmaline, garnet, and corundum (ruby), but such specimens are very rare and of interest only to the collector looking for the unusual or exotic. We hope, rather, to have given the reader a broad spectrum of the kinds of materials the Chinese conquered with the use of imagination, artistic ability, and simple tools.

15
Dating Jade Objects

The Chinese have created jade objects for more than thirty-five hundred years. Yet few reign marks or meaningful inscriptions have been found on them, except on those made to carry important messages, such as the two jade books recently acquired by the Palace Museum in Taipei (see Ills. 21–24). Not until the eighteenth century, when Emperor Ch'ien-lung, the indefatigable versifier and calligraphist, ascended the throne, did reign marks and inscriptions become a regular feature on the monumental pieces produced in the palace. Then the technique of cutting characters with a diamond instrument became an important one with the palace jade workers.*

Unlike porcelain, another favorite of Western collectors, jade is extremely difficult to date. It takes little effort for potters or decorators to add reign marks or inscriptions to their products, and such has been their custom since the end of the Sung dynasty (A.D. 960–1279). With the aid of an authentic reign mark and other factors, a piece of porcelain can sometimes be correctly dated to the exact year or at least to within a quarter of a century.

---

*We can credit the emperor with the first use of diamond tools in incising verses and reign marks. The diamond was known to the author of the *Ko Ku Yao Lun* (1388), in which the gem was mentioned as being able to drill a hole in a Tingware bowl. Apparently it was not used in jade work at the time of his writing. Had it been used, he would have mentioned it.

Not so, jade. During the Chou dynasty (1122–221 B.C.), when inscriptions on bronze vessels ran to several hundreds of words, and when the technique of jade carving had achieved such sophistication as free rings and extensive piercing, inscriptions on jade were rarely attempted. Only a few archaic jades have been found with carved characters. The reason may be that Chinese calligraphy is an art—in fact, the highest form of art—and it was impossible to fulfill the artistic standards of calligraphy on such an intractable material as jade. We are thus denied the most important aid in dating jade objects. Only by analyzing the following factors can we hope to attack the dating problem.

1. The availability of raw material: Before jadeite came on the scene during the eighteenth century, China depended upon Khotan and Yarkand for her supply of jade even more than the United States now depends upon the Middle East for oil. Any obstruction on the long and difficult caravan route dried up the supply. This happened several times in the course of history.

2. Patronage of the ruling class: Jade, during the first thousand years of Chinese history, was, unlike porcelain, strictly a product for the ruling class.

3. Any drastic change in the country due to non-Chinese domination.

4. Technical development: Technical changes, rapid at certain times, stagnant at others, are another aid to dating.

5. Motifs and designs: There is a definite relationship between the motifs and designs on jade objects and those used in other arts and crafts. Although the motifs from earlier ages were repeated, there are differences, however small, between objects produced at different periods.

Dating problems can be better understood if one has some historical perspective.

The Archaic Period

From the Shang dynasty to the end of the Chou dynasty or the Warring States period (1766–221 B.C.), jade was used for ceremonial or sacrificial purposes, as insignia of the various ranks of nobles, for making scientific or astronomical instruments, and for personal adornment (see Appendix). During the short Warring States period, the feudal system began to disintegrate. The powerful princes and dukes wanted their lapidaries to produce all the jade objects that formerly only the king could possess or bestow upon his nobles. This unusual patronage resulted in great advances in carving techniques. They were not excelled except by the Ch'ien-lung period, nearly two thousand years later.

The treasured jade objects beloved by the powerful noblemen during their lives followed them into their graves. (The belief in an afterlife was important in Chinese culture from the earliest times.) Actually, the burial of jade objects with the dead became a necessity during the Han period (206 B.C.–A.D. 220) because the Taoist and astrological schools promoted the belief that jade had the power to preserve the corpse and give protection to the soul of the deceased until the time of the resurrection. The prestige of the Han dynasty was high. Constant campaigns, both military and diplomatic, kept the bordering nations and tribes aware of its influence. The supply of jade was plentiful. Most excavated tomb jades are crudely carved, but they show that people could afford to use this hitherto prohibitively expensive raw material for objects that would be interred and never seen again. Artistically speaking, designs of naturalistic objects began to appear during this period, a marked departure from the stylized patterns that carvers had faithfully followed heretofore.

Thanks to the efforts of both Chinese and Western scholars, and controlled excavations during the last seventy-five years, we know more now about archaic jade than we did at any previous time, so we can be reasonably confident in assigning a jade piece to "Shang," "Shang or early Chou," "Spring and Autumn period," "Warring States period," and "Han." (For illustrations, see Appendix.) Designs (or the lack of any), shapes, and forms give the best clues. Most archaic jades are flat; it was the custom at that time to cut the raw material first into slabs. The motifs are mostly mythological (their counterparts can be found on the bronze vessels of the identical periods); also among them were favorite hunting animals, first extremely stylized, then more naturalistic.

It is important that the smallest detail should not be overlooked. Holes on the early archaic jades—most early jades do have them—were conical,

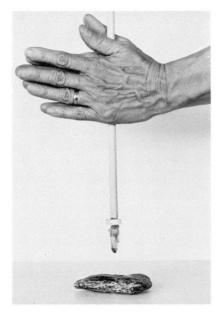

194. The earliest holes were probably made with wedge-shaped quartz crystals of various sizes.

probably made by turning a wedge-shaped tool, most likely a sharp quartz crystal attached to a stick. The stick could be kept turning in the open palms with a back and forth movement. Some scholars think that the earlier conical holes were made by bamboo drills, with quartz sand as an abrasive, and that those on the later pieces are more uniform because iron had been discovered and made into drills. This may be so. However, we think the conical holes might be the result of a wobbly vertical drill—a simple contraption consisting of a round stick put through a hole in the middle of a horizontal bar, with a rope or string fastened to one end of the stick and tied to the two extremities of the horizontal bar. The drill bit, of either bamboo or iron, was attached to the other end of the round stick. It was as simple a tool as the potter's wheel, which had been in use since prehistoric times. By winding the rope a few times in one direction and applying a steady rhythmical pressure, this primitive drill would keep turning first one way and then the other, and accomplish the drilling. In any case, bamboo is as good a carrier of abrasive as iron, and perhaps just as lasting.

As long as a hole or holes were needed—for instance, to tie the jade to a handle—a conical hole would serve the purpose. However, it would not do for a jade that was to be hung loose, as in a set of musical stones. Then the smaller end of the conical hole, regardless of whether it was made by a bamboo or iron drill, would have to be enlarged, so that the jade piece or pieces would hang in the desired position. It is also true that a vertical drill with a section of bamboo of small diameter would be a good tool to carve or polish the grain patterns so common on the archaic jades. In any event, since no early lapidary tools have been found or have been identified as such, all arguments, pro and con, must be considered as speculative only.

It is important to know that during the Sung (960–1279) and the Ming (1368–1644) dynasties, the neoclassical periods, in which ancient sacrificial and ceremonial rites were performed, ritualistic bronze vessels and jade objects were much copied and used. These semiarchaic objects have far less value than have the genuine archaic objects. How does one tell the difference between the two? That's a question that cannot be answered in a nutshell. Generally speaking, because of the fact that fewer archaic specimens were available for research at those times (Sung and Ming), semiarchaic jades often show a departure from or misrepresentation of archaic motifs. If the reader wants to become expert in recognizing archaic jade, he should go to a museum that has a large collection, and spend days and days there comparing and memorizing until he develops a sixth sense for telling the archaic from the semiarchaic and, more importantly, the faked archaic.

Unfortunately, not only during the last fifty years but right now, thousands and thousands of faked archaic jade objects have been and are being made out of low-grade jade or, more often, serpentine, and sold as genuine archaic jade. For instance, at almost any antiques shop you can buy a cicada with flared wings made from a waterish light green serpentine with brown spots that suggest the look of calcification or alteration.

The Medieval Period

In studying this long period—call it the medieval, if you will—scholars trying to date jade flounder like a captain trying to sail a ship without a compass. It started with the Six Dynasties (or the Northern and Southern dynasties: A.D. 265–589), when the northern tribes occupied the most civilized part of China, and the educated and influential Chinese fled south of the Yangtze River. There was a drastic shift in the country's religious and philosophical beliefs, and much slaughter; the people were steeped in misery. Buddhism, with its preaching of mercy and compassion, was eagerly embraced by the Chinese. All their energy went into creating stone Buddhist statues and steles. Even though the jade-producing region was friendly to the tribes that ruled China, the art of jade carving suffered neglect. Jade objects that can be tentatively identified as belonging to this period are animals in naturalistic forms, often carved in the round, and odd non-Chinese human figures—the type of designs that the barbarous rulers appreciated. Obviously, merely having a plentiful supply of raw jade was not enough to stimulate greater activity, although lack of material certainly can stifle the art.

With the reunification of China by the T'ang dynasty (A.D. 618–907), preceded by the short Sui dynasty (A.D. 581–618), China ushered in her second glorious historical period. Her power and prestige again extended over the borders. The supply of raw jade was no problem. The rulers of the T'ang dynasty were cosmopolitan in taste. Mideastern gold and silver work was appreciated as much as were China's own unique products. Jade carvers, however—although they were able to revive the art after long neglect—failed to make it one of their greatest periods. The jade objects produced in this period seem somewhat bulky, even clumsy. The refinement achieved and cherished during the Warring States period was no longer present.

After another split, into the Five Dynasties (A.D. 907–960), China was reunited. The Sung dynasty (960–1279) was inherently weak and its territory small, and the supply of jade was uncertain and difficult to obtain. Yet, because of the prevailing respect for classical learning and the cultural heritage, the art of jade carving seems to have regained its ancient esteem and patronage. Great efforts were made to achieve perfection, using classical shapes, forms, and designs as models. The Sung emperors were great patrons of the traditional arts, some of them great artists in their own right.

Then the Mongols conquered China and established the short-lived Yüan dynasty (A.D. 1277–1368). They were a warlike people—their only interest was to add more territory to their domain. The very few objects that are recognized as Yüan jade are limited to such ungainly things as the famous gigantic dragon wine jar, which the Emperor Ch'ien-lung rescued from a monastery where it was being used as a pickle container. Yet during this dynasty the supply of raw jade was certainly sufficient to meet any demand.

195. White jade mountain, with figures climbing the lonely path. *Stanford University Museum*

The Ming dynasty (A.D. 1368–1644) was a "replay" of the Sung dynasty, with the same respect for the traditional philosophy and arts. Jade carving again received stimulus from the ruling class, and there was noticeable progress in technique and design, especially during the late Ming period. Naturalistic designs, particularly those intimately related to the Taoist ideal of longevity and immortality, or those with the felicity of hidden meanings (rebuses or word puns) were favored. This trend reached its peak during the reign of Chia-ching (1522–1566), who, in forty years, paid no attention to national affairs but devoted all his time to the pursuit of longevity.

We are not at the end of the nightmarishly long period (fifteen hundred years!) in which dating jade is no better than hit or miss. The best thing any scholar can say is "This seems to be a T'ang piece or earlier" (a span of three hundred years or more!) or "This looks like Sung, but it could be early Ming" (a span of five hundred years!). Museums have been dating and redating specimens from this period, and they often must add question marks to their dating. Comparing motifs and designs with those on porcelain, cloisonné, and other objects sometimes, but not always, offers clues. The jade carver, limited by the material he had to work with, had constantly to bear in mind that he must not waste the expensive stone. He was thus not always free to do what he wanted. Just as the primitive Shang jade worker had to find the right shape of pebble to make into a bird, even the modern carver, with all the sophisticated tools at his command, is still hampered by the same restriction. Hence, a gray white boulder already suggesting the shape of a mountain is a candidate for a jade mountain. The carver will need only to select the proper places to carve in relief a thatched house covered by the low branches of an old pine tree, a mountain path, and perhaps one or two scholars or hermits to supply human interest. If he chooses instead to make a slender graceful statue of Kwan-yin, the Goddess of Mercy, he will not turn out a successful piece because the color will be drab and the face splotchy, and he will also do a lot of unnecessary cutting, which is time-consuming and wasteful of precious material.

Finally, Chinese collectors and connoisseurs are essentially conservative. Jade carvers who create objects for their enjoyment are likely to repeat the motifs and designs most admired in earlier times. Therefore, certain characteristics must be considered in the context of the spirit of the age—namely, the barbarous or, rather, non-Chinese taste for the vigorous and realistic during the Six Dynasties, the gaiety and exuberance of the T'ang, the restraint of Sung and Ming, and the preference for overdecoration, ungainly shapes, and large size of the Yüan.

The Modern Age

The great modern age began with Emperor K'ang-hsi (1662–1722) of the newly established Manchu dynasty or, even earlier, with the late Ming period (sixteenth century to early in the first half of the seventeenth century), and culminated during the reign of Ch'ien-lung (1736–95), under whose patronage and encouragement jade carvers not only recaptured the technical sophistication of the Warring States period nearly two thousand years earlier, but surpassed it. Jade carving, emerging from the long medieval period, definitely established itself as a branch of Chinese art. The supply of raw jade, both nephrite and jadeite, became more than plentiful. Not only the palace atelier, but the large workshops in Peking, Soochow, and Canton, worked on nothing but jade of the finest grade. Ch'ien-lung's taste was cosmopolitan. Jade vessels with paper-thin walls and embellished with rubies, emeralds, and sapphires in the Indian and Tibetan style were also copied in his palace workshops. But the delicate and clever reticulation left no doubt that the objects could be produced only by Chinese hands. The emperor even ordered some important archaic jades to be recarved and incised with inscriptions—as questionable a practice as perfuming a rose or adding another hue to the rainbow.

Since Ch'ien-lung's time, the art of jade carving has continued to enjoy popularity. Today, decorative items such as ring cabochons, bracelets, and pendants made from jadeite of very attractive colors are produced in great numbers and available to jade lovers at very reasonable prices. They are machine-cut but finished by hand. Some, however, are smoothed and polished in tumblers, and then the prices are even cheaper.

Two main factors contributed to increased production of jade objects at the turn of the present century: the inventions of the inexpensive abrasive Carborundum, with a hardness of 9.*, and of the electrically operated lathe with its great variety of attachments to do the rough cutting and precision carving and polishing. However, there is no substitute for the skill of human hands in guiding the tools—actually, guiding the rough jade to the fixed tools. Recently one of the biggest American dealers and collectors (see "Curio Notes" in *Arts of Asia,* vol. 6, no. 1) was invited to see the carvers at work in mainland China. He was told that it still takes three days to cut a free ring and another three days to polish it. To many people in the Western world, jade carving seems a foolish way of wasting time, but to the Chinese, time is of little concern. They seem to love to do things the hard way. They paint pictures inside a tiny glass snuff bottle, sometimes depicting up to two hundred people, and take six months to complete the work. They build layer upon layer of lacquer of various colors until it is a half-inch thick, and then carve landscapes and floral patterns in it, exposing the different colors. Each of the seventy or eighty layers of lacquer takes three or four days to dry before another coat can be applied. Such a piece takes a year to finish. This is one reason that oriental antiques fetch such high prices.

Since jade is so difficult to date accurately, we want to remind our readers that when a dealer offers a jade as T'ang or Sung or Ming, the wise collector will take the statement with a big handful of salt, and refuse to be influenced by the sales pitch. Actually, a person need not worry about dating jade until he has collected for several years and formed the intention of specializing in it. Then he should accumulate the necessary knowledge by visiting museums and reading with discrimination all the material he can find. Needless to say, *handling* is most important—he should handle jade whenever he has the chance.

But even a beginning collector should know how to judge a piece of jade. This is largely a personal matter, like choosing a bride. First, the intrinsic beauty of the stone has to be considered. Second, one must judge the quality of the workmanship, from the overall design down to the finishing touches, the smoothing out of all the rough cuts, and an overall polishing of the high and low points. A good jade piece, like a good bride, is a finished embodiment of beauty.

Above all, the beginner must be sure that what he buys as jade *is* jade, either nephrite or jadeite. Too often, a dealer mutters peevishly, when a customer wants to do a scratch test, "I don't want my beautiful jade to be scratched." How can he expect a buyer to tell by eyes alone that it is not serpentine or even soapstone, and to pay the price he asks? Instead, an honest dealer should offer his pocketknife, point out a smoothly polished

---

*In earlier times, forty-two different kinds of abrasives were used. The most important ones were crushed quartz, garnet, corundum (black sand), and ruby crystals.

spot under the base or on the back of the piece, and invite the customer to make the test. (Many dealers have done just that for us.)

We like the practice of Keller and Scott of Carmel, California. Once they bought a large collection. The original owner had been rather indiscriminate in making his acquisitions, and about 20 percent of them were bowenite or other hard stones. The partners thereupon went to work and carefully tested every piece, then labeled them either as jade, bowenite, serpentine, or other material, and guaranteed them as such. In no time, the whole collection was sold.

Jade is still relatively new to the American public. It is to the dealers' benefit to give interested would-be customers all the facts, and all the assurances they can.

Variables Affecting the Art of Jade Carving

Major Historical Periods	Supply of Raw Jade	Non-Chinese Domination or Influence	Technical Advancement	Production
Shang 1766 ? B.C.–1122 B.C.				
Chou 1122 B.C.–221 B.C. (Warring States: 481 B.C.–221 B.C.)				
Han 206 B.C.–A.D. 220				
Six Dynasties 285–589				
T'ang 618–907				
Sung 960–1279				
Yuan 1277–1368				
Ming 1368–1644				
Ch'in 1644–1912				

Appendix

Archaic Jade *(Ills. 196–201)*

The illustrations herein depict the best known of the archaic jade forms.

Ceremonial Jades and Tallies

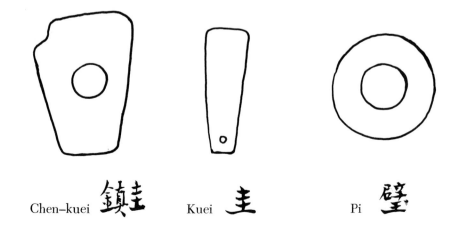

Chen–kuei 鎭圭 Kuei 圭 Pi 璧

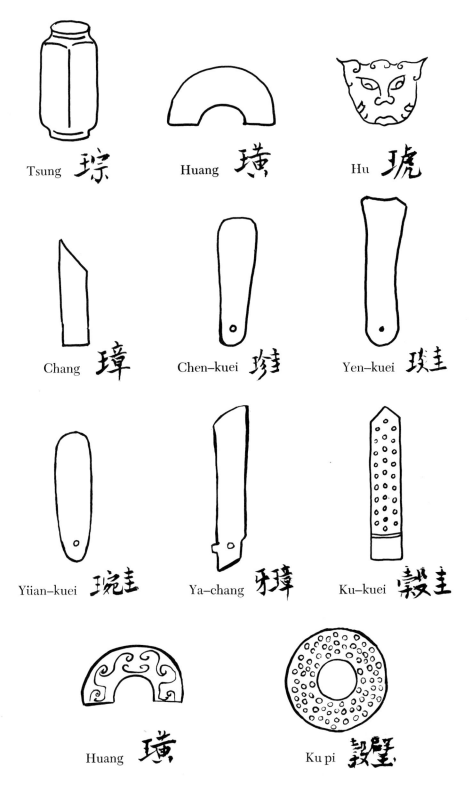

Tsung 琮

Huang 璜

Hu 琥

Chang 璋

Chen–kuei 珍

Yen–kuei 琰圭

Yüan–kuei 琬圭

Ya–chang 牙璋

Ku–kuei 穀圭

Huang 璜

Ku pi 穀璧

Astronomical Instrument

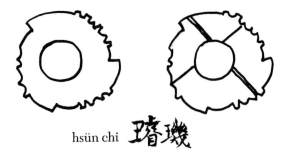

hsün chi 璿璣

Symbols of Heavenly Bodies, Mountains, and Rivers

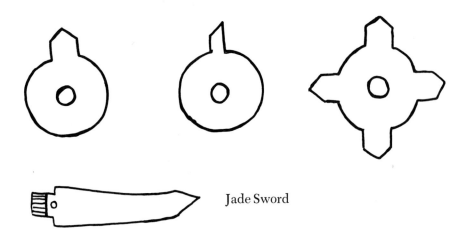

Jade Sword

Jade Ceremonial Weapons

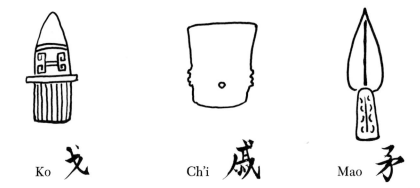

Ko 戈   Ch'i 戚   Mao 矛

Sword Furniture

peng 琫

sui 璲

wei 璏

pi 珌

Belt—inlaid pieces in front

Jade Ornaments

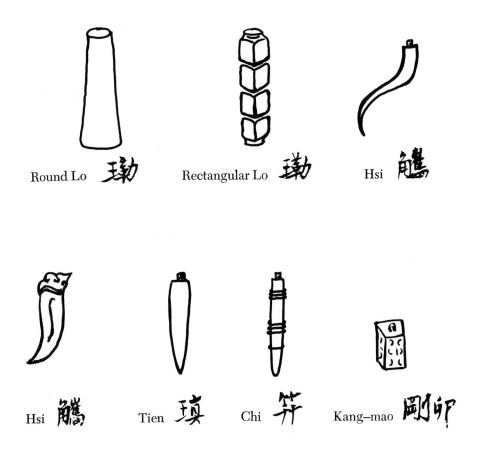

Round Lo 瑓   Rectangular Lo 瑓   Hsi 觿

Hsi 觿   Tien 瑱   Chi 笄   Kang–mao 剛卯

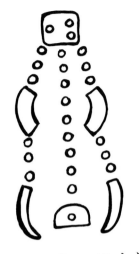

Set of Jade 古玉瑚文全佩
Musical Stones
(Girdle Pendant)

Funerary Jades 慎目

Musical Stone 玉磬

202. Jade burial suit of Tou Wan, wife of Liu Sheng,
Prince of Chungshan. Han dynasty. This suit was
unearthed at Mancheng, in China's Hopei Province,
in 1968, by the People's Republic of China.

A Comment On Jade Prices

Knowing that readers are usually disappointed not to find a price list to consult, and that publishers like to include price information lest a book be ignominiously labeled in retailers' catalogs as NPL (no price list), we will do our best to provide some basic realistic information about the problem of prices. However, we will not attempt the impossible—to provide specific prices for specific pieces.

Veteran compilers of price lists insist that they do not themselves "make up" prices, but merely collect and collate the asking prices at antiques shows, shops, auctions, and various advertised sales, and feed these into a computer. Then, presto: out comes a list of "official prices"! Unfortunately, in the case of jade, many sellers don't know "a hawk from a handsaw." Serpentine, bowenite, soapstone, and other minerals are often—by honest mistake or false hope—labeled "jade." And if this type of misinformation is fed into the finest computer ever built, the old rule will still hold true: "Garbage in—garbage out."

Generally speaking, archaic jades cannot be priced at all, particularly the rare types with no damage, such as the Hsün Chi on our dust jacket. Their price is a matter between the connoisseur and the dealer, or between one connoisseur and another. When an agreement is reached, the price is right. Archaic jades have the quality or "mystique" that cannot be measured in terms of dollars.

Jade objects of the long medieval period, from the third century to the sixteenth or seventeenth centuries, also have that quality of mystique, but in a descending scale. It is still difficult, if not impossible, to price them, although the color and purity of the jade and the artistry of the carving become important considerations as we get closer to the Ch'ien-lung period.

In judging jades carved after the eighteenth century, there are three main criteria to consider (they apply to both nephrite and jadeite; the latter was fast gaining in popularity at the time):

1. The material: its degree of translucency and the absence of any fracture or blemish.

2. The color: The purist considers nephrite as the "real Chinese jade." Nothing thrills him more than an old jade object carved out of the unctuous, pure, and white mutton-fat jade. Tastes change, however, and since 90 percent of carved jade is now Burmese jadeite, we can no longer look to the *Ko Ku Yao Lun* (written in 1388) for guidance. Good greens lead in popularity in either jewelry or large carvings. Next is mauve or lavender. Yellow is rare, and therefore is priced as high, or sometimes even higher. True red, the color of a ripe tomato, is rarely seen except in tiny patches, but there are plenty of reddish brown examples, particularly in jadeite. This color often shows up directly under the skin of jade boulders.

3. Artistic design, carving technique, and effective exploitation of the varied colors within each piece.

The important thing to remember, however, is that the reason (reasons) you fall in love with a piece of jade is a most personal thing that cannot be explained. Just as "friendship is above reason," your feeling for your favorite jade often increases as you discover more beauty—or even imperfections—in the stone. A translucent, delicate mauve and green maiden may symbolize ideal womanhood—or your long-lost first love. A pendant that was a gift from a now-deceased friend may be enhanced in value by the memories attached to it; and the little jade animal on your table may have become as much a pet and companion as a live one would have been. So who is to say where intrinsic value ends and sentiment and personal attachment begin?

Remember, too, that owners almost never sell their favorite jades if they can avoid doing so. It's their heirs who put such beloved treasures on the auction block.

203. Jade screens shown in *Arts of Asia* magazine, January–February 1977. *Courtesy of* Arts of Asia *and Sotheby Parke Bernet (Hong Kong) Ltd.*

Collectors interested in large specimens can pick up a magazine like *Arts of Asia*, where all the important jades sold at international auctions, such as Sotheby Parke Bernet and Christie's, are shown in vivid color. After the sale, the auctioneer's estimates and the actual selling prices are reported. Both the above-mentioned auction houses, like many others, publish catalogs that the collector can obtain.

The stock market cynic says that the small investor is always wrong. However, collecting involves more than investment; it also represents a satisfaction of one's artistic longings, an appreciation of interesting and beautiful objects. Here, the small collector—one who cares enough to study and learn—can often be as "right" as, or even more right than, the giants with millions to spend. In the first place, a small collector with limited funds counts his dollars and cents, does his legwork, and constantly upgrades his collection by trading for better specimens. The giants, on the other hand, often buy things sight unseen through agents who fly around the world to attend all the big auctions and who are amply rewarded for their expertise and globe-trotting.

To see how one can start with a small budget of twenty-five to a hundred dollars, refer back to the chapter on jade flowers. The People's Republic of China has so many girdle pendants, hair pins, and jade flowers "donated by the people" that they are willing to sell them—or, literally, dump them on the market—at the Canton Trade Fair. The price for these things is at an all-time low. One can buy exquisitely carved jade flowers, as well as pendants, thumb rings, belt hooks, and the like, from dealers such as Mrs. Palmer (see Chapter 6, "Jade—Our Common Language"), who are willing to make a small profit, perhaps as little as a couple of inflated and devaluated dollars, in some instances.

Some of the small items may be a few hundred years old. The Chinese do not have enough experts available to examine the millions of these small pieces that are packaged and sold in lots. One of the authors of this essay spent half his lifetime in China, but cannot recall that they were *that* cheap thirty or forty years ago. Americans who lived in China in the 1920s and 1930s will confirm that statement. Of course many of the pieces are chipped or broken, but Chapter 9 (on carving your own jade) will show you how to correct most small imperfections by sanding, and how to restore damaged old pieces to their original beauty.

To repeat (and this is worth repeating over and over again), for assessing a piece of jade the rule of thumb is: Judge by the quality of the material (its purity, translucence, color—the fewer blemishes, fractures, and inclusions, the better) and the workmanship (the amount of skilled and even talented carving, the time, mental concentration, and effort involved). A lot of clumsy drilling and incising means nothing.

As we write this, a fluted jadeite dish comes to mind. Carved paper-thin, with harmonious undulations, it was beautifully designed in a pleasing, irregularly oblong shape, about two by three inches, and polished to perfection. The dish was, to borrow a ceramic term, "bodiless," light as the notes produced by a master violinist. It was shown to us by a lady who attended one of our lectures.

"Do you know how much it's worth?" she asked.

"If it were ours, no money could buy it."

"How much do you think I paid for it?" she persisted.

"We wouldn't know that, either. Perhaps quite a lot."

"Well," the woman went on, proud and pleased, "I paid just a dollar for it."

"Really! But when?"

"About seventeen years ago. I was in a Chinese import store—the young owner was selling out the inventory after his father's death. He asked only a dollar because it has a small fracture line on it. See?"

"Oh, yes." We could hardly see the line. "It really doesn't matter very much."

That lovely dish still lives on in our memory—it will probably always haunt us with its beauty.

If you are just beginning to be interested in collecting jade, the first and most important consideration is to make sure that what you pay for as jade *is* actually jade.

Recently, a dealer who had been at the Canton Trade Fair (held in the spring and fall of each year) showed us several dozen beautifully carved serpentine and/or bowenite figurines and vessels of the monumental category (in jadeology, "monumental" means anything from six to ten or more inches), each contained in a satin-lined, brocade-covered box. The prices ranged from $250 to $750. When the dealer saw that we didn't jump at them, he made his sales pitch, and a rather low-pressure one, at that: "You don't have to worry that they are *not* jade. I was in China just two months ago, and I can assure you they do business on the principle of strict honesty and integrity."

"We agree with you absolutely," we told him. "After all, none of these boxes bears the word 'jade' in either Chinese or English!"

Bibliography

The following books represent only a small number of those published on the subject of jade. Readability has been our primary concern. A book that cannot be read through and enjoyed does not increase the collector's interest. If an informative book happens to have many fine pictures in black and white or, better still, in vivid true color, so much the better. We do not dismiss highly pictorial presentations as mere coffee-table books.

Periodicals were chosen for the same reasons, as well as for their timeliness.

Chinese books, both old and recently published, are good sources for research. However, no attempt has been made to list them unless they are easily available in English versions.

Books

Bauer, Max. *Precious Stones*, vol. 2 (first published in 1904). New York: Dover Publications Inc., 1968.

Cheng, Te-k'un. *Jade Flowers and Floral Patterns in Chinese Decorative Art*. Hong Kong: Carlson Printers, Ltd., 1969.

David, Sir Percival, trans. and ed. *Chinese Connoisseurship—The Ko Ku Yao Lun, The Essential Criteria of Antiquities* (with a facsimile of the Chinese text of 1388). London: Faber and Faber, 1971.

Hansford, S. Howard. *Chinese Carved Jades*. Greenwich, Conn.: New York Graphic Society, 1968.

Kennedy, Gordon, et al. *The Fundamentals of Gemstone Carving*. San Diego, California: Lapidary Journal Inc., 1967.

Laufer, Berthold. *Jade, A Study in Chinese Archaelogy and Religion* (first published in Chicago in 1912). New York: Dover Publications, Inc., 1974.

National Palace Museum Illustrated Handbook, Chinese Cultural Art Treasures. Taipei, Taiwan: The National Palace Museum, Republic of China, 1967.

Nott, Stanley Charles. *Chinese Jade Throughout the Ages* (first published in 1936). Rutland, Vermont, and Tokyo, Japan: Charles Tuttle Co., 1973.

Ruff, Elsie. *Jade of the Maori*. London: F.J. Milner and Sons Ltd., 1950.

Snowman, A. Kenneth. *The Art of Carl Fabergé*. London: Faber and Faber, 1953.

Strachey, Giles Lytton. *Eminent Victorians*. New York: The Modern Library, 1918.

Wills, Geoffrey. *Jade, A Collectors Guide*. South Brunswick, New York: A.S. Barnes and Co. Inc., 1964.

——. *Jade of the East*. New York: John Weatherhill Publications, Inc., 1972.

Zara, Louis. *Jade*. New York: Walker and Co., 1969.

Magazines, Periodicals, Pamphlets

Allen, Jamey. "Amber and Its Substitutes." *Bead Journal*, vol. 2, no. 3; vol. 2, no. 4; vol. 3, no. 1.

Ashley, Robin. "Jade Man Down Under." *Arts of Asia*, vol. 3, no. 2, March–April 1973.

Desautels, Paul E. "Jade Is a Mystery 4,000 Years Old That Transcends Science." *Smithsonian*, April 1977.

Gwinn, Ethel. "Lizzadro Museum." *Arts of Asia*, vol. 4, no. 6, November–December 1974.

Hartman, Joan. "The Bishop Jade Collection." *Arts of Asia*, vol. 4, no. 3, May–June 1974.

Hemrich, Gerald I. "Jade." *Gembooks*, Mentone, California, 1966.

Keverne, Roger. "Jade, A Review of the Exhibition at the Victoria and Albert Museum, London." *Arts of Asia*, vol. 5, no. 4, July–August 1975.

Leary, R. H. "Jade Mine in Canada." *Arts of Asia*, vol. 3, no. 5, September–October 1973.

Mallory, Lester D. "Jadeite in Middle America." *Lapidary Journal*, December 1971.

Markbreiter, Stephen. "Chu's." *Arts of Asia*, vol. 4, no. 6, November–December 1974.

Nguyet, Tuyet. "Edward Dominik: Interview." *Arts of Asia*, vol. 3, no. 2, March–April 1973.

Zahl, Paul A. " Golden Window on the Past." *National Geographic Magazine*, vol. 152, no. 3, September 1977 (amber mining in Dominican Republic).

Zhi-ren, Qu. "Jade in Ancient China." *Arts of Asia*, vol. 1, no. 1, January–February 1971.

Index

(Note: *References to illustration numbers are in italics*)